More Pra

THIS TRUTH NEVE~

"David Rynick is a master of the koans of everyday life."
—Barry Magid, author of *Ending the Pursuit of Happiness*

"A loving book that makes you happy when you pick it
up and read any chapter."
—John Tarrant, author of *Bring Me the Rhinoceros and
Other Zen Koans That Will Save Your Life*

"Beautifully written."
—Cheryl Wilfong, author of *The Meditative Gardener*

"Heartfelt and delightful."
—Ronald D. Siegel, author of *The Mindfulness Solution*

"I love this book! It's intimate, honest, real.
A book to be savored a few pages at a time."
—Frank Jude Boccio, author of *Mindfulness Yoga*

"A gentle and lovely companion for our journey."
—Rafe Martin, author of *Endless Path*
and *The Banyan Deer*

"Compelling and deeply touching."
—Lin Jensen, author of *Bad Dog!* and *Deep Down Things*

"A map to treasures of unsurpassable value—
the extraordinary miracles that may be found in ordinary
moments of life."
—Steve Flowers, author of
The Mindful Path through Shyness

"These scenes from Rynick's book are teaching stories
that take us straight back to love."
—Susan Moon, author of *This Is Getting Old*

"David's love of nature, his warmth and compassion, his
full humanity, shine forth on every page."
—Paul Ropp, author of *China in World History*

"Delightful! David Rynick shares his personal story with
disarming honesty, vulnerability, beauty, and humor.
Rich and accessible."
—Claude Stein, director of the Natural Singer Workshop

"This book had me laughing out loud, and crying, all
while filling me with wonder. A deeply intimate book—
and an elegant and rich offering worthy of savoring."
—Faith Fuller, Ph.D., founder of
CRR Global coaching school

"A lovely reminder of the simple essence of an aware life."
—Rev. Dr. Terasa G. Cooley,
director for congregational life,
Unitarian Universalist Association

This Truth Never Fails

A ZEN MEMOIR IN FOUR SEASONS

David Rynick

Wisdom Publications • Boston

Wisdom Publications
199 Elm Street
Somerville MA 02144 USA
www.wisdompubs.org

Library of Congress Cataloging-in-Publication Data

Rynick, David.
This truth never fails : a Zen memoir in four seasons / David Rynick.
pages cm
Includes bibliographical references and index.
ISBN 1-61429-008-3 (pbk. : alk. paper)
1. Rynick, David. 2. Spiritual biography. 3. Zen Buddhism. I. Title.
BQ982.Y65A3 2012
294.3'927092—dc23
[B]
2011048872

ISBN 978-1-61429-008-7
eBook ISBN 978-1-61429-024-7

16 15 14 13 12
5 4 3 2 1

Illustrations by Richard Wehrman. Cover design by Richard Wehrman. Interior design
by Gopa&Ted2. Set in Dante MT Std 11.5/16. Author photo by Todd Curtis.

Wisdom Publications' books are printed on acid-free paper and meet the guidelines
for permanence and durability of the Production Guidelines for Book
Longevity of the Council on Library Resources.

Printed in the United States of America.

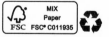

This book was produced with environmental mindfulness. We have elected to
print this title on 30% PCW recycled paper. As a result, we have saved the follow-
ing resources: 19 trees, 9 million BTUs of energy, 1,880 lbs. of greenhouse 8,478
gallons of water, and 537 lbs. of solid waste. For more information, please visit
our website, www.wisdompubs.org. This paper is also FSC® certified. For more
information, please visit www.fscus.org.

to Melissa

Table of Contents

Winter

Spring

Introduction

When I look deeply into the real form of the universe,
everything reveals the mysterious truth of the Buddha.
This truth never fails: in every moment and every place,
things can't help but shine with this light.
—TOREI ENJI

I COULD BLAME my involvement in Zen on my parents. My dad was a Presbyterian minister who believed we should look for God in the midst of our ordinary lives. My mom, a less overtly "spiritual" person, was endlessly appreciative of the wonders and beauty of the everyday world. So when I encountered Zen Buddhism in my early twenties, the teachings sounded like what I had been hearing all my life: what is most precious and sacred is right here—all we have to do is turn toward it.

My commitment to the path of Zen is also an expression of a deep yearning for connection that has been with me all my life. This persistent longing—which has so often felt like a problem—has been the compass of my life. When I heard a Zen teacher talk in 1980, he spoke of what I knew in my bones—that though we often experience ourselves as separate and suffering individuals, we are also lovingly held in a vast and luminous web of aliveness.

And I believed him when he said there is a direct path toward waking up to this aliveness.

The path of Zen is not about leaving the world behind or getting something we don't already have. This path of awakening "simply" requires stopping our incessant busyness and our fervent searching long enough to be able to receive what is already abundantly here. Easier said than done, of course, and so this is where formal meditation practice comes in.

WHEN WE SIT IN ZEN MEDITATION, we're not trying to rid ourselves of thoughts nor are we cultivating exalted states of mind. We're practicing the surprisingly difficult work of being who we already are—cultivating a basic friendliness toward ourselves and our experience. Over time, the discipline of meditation can help us grow in our capacity to appreciate the aliveness of each moment, regardless of the content.

But the point of Zen is not about perfecting the art of sitting still. The real-time complexity of our everyday lives is where our most challenging (and rewarding) practice takes place. Zen does not offer a magical escape from the ups and downs of our lives. However, as we learn to meet what is arising with curiosity and compassion, the quality of our ordinary lives is transformed. Even in the midst of the flood of events, emotions, and thoughts, we find something genuinely trustworthy. We stop looking somewhere else and begin to participate more intimately in the truth of this life we already have. Right here, in these exact circumstances.

THIS COLLECTION of short observations and reflections is my "Zen memoir"—a record of my ongoing practice and study of this extraordinary experience we call ordinary life. While written over a period of several years, I have arranged these pieces into the cycle of the seasons of a single year. Each piece stands alone but is also part of a loose overall narrative that includes leaving a home of eighteen years and creating a Zen temple in a lovely old Victorian mansion where I now live, meditate, and teach with my wife Melissa Myozen Blacker, also a Zen teacher.

In the process of writing, I have been increasingly aware that when we talk or write, we are never wholly reporting on something outside ourselves. Each perception and each description is an interpretation, a creation of the moment based on bits of information. In some of these reflections I stick quite closely to what others might be able to verify. In other pieces I have allowed myself to wander far afield—to dream into what I see and hear and feel. This dreaming is one way of presenting what Zen Master Kosho Uchiyama means when he says, "Everything you encounter is your life." Each encounter is both meeting the eternal Other—what is always outside and unknown—and meeting ourselves in the particular form of the moment.

When I truly hear the hoarse call of the starlings on the birdfeeder, the calling and the hearing become one thing and I find my way into the world where "I" and the starlings are not as separate as it might appear.

At the heart of things, there is a truth that is always revealing itself. Whether we call it the Dharma, or God, or the universe, or aliveness—it is essentially ungraspable. In these writings, I use these names and others as a stand-in for this essence that can never be truly named. But though the true source of our lives is beyond words, we can surely know and come to rely on this mysterious truth.

All of us have had moments, however brief, when we catch a glimpse of the beauty and wonder that surrounds us, that *is* us. The smell of petunias on a clear June morning, the spontaneous hug of a toddler, the notes of a melody that resonate in our deepest heart, the loving eyes of a friend. In these moments nothing more needs to be said. A smile appears, our eyes brim with tears, we nod in silent recognition.

What we long for is always present, hiding in plain sight. Every situation we encounter contains the truth of our existence. Utterly reliable and always ungraspable, we are never separate from this mysterious aliveness.

My hope is that these reflections will remind you of what you already know and awaken your heart more deeply to the luminous possibility inherent in each moment of every life.

SUMMER

First Day Back

MONDAY MORNING—I wake up groggy after a week's vacation. It's only 5:30—no need to get up yet. I doze lightly till 6:00 when the urge to pee becomes irresistible. I shuffle to the bathroom, do my business, then slip back between the sheets. A humid night and the warm air already feels oppressive. There's no drifting back to sleep this morning. I lay here—at the beginning of my day, in the middle of my life—and work with my brain that has already begun to scan the horizon for news of trouble. As usual, there's an abundance available.

My anxious morning mind is like a young dog out for a walk. Every tree and every bush must be investigated to find out who's peed there and what the news is. The objects of my worrying investigation this morning are many. The garden is running wild—so many things to be tied up or weeded or dug up and moved. The to-do list in preparation for the next retreat and the workers that may or may not be coming today to repair the newly discovered leak in the roof. Then there is my life-coaching business—do I have enough clients? Will the next workshop really happen? And I should have replaced my website years ago—I can usually ignore this undone task, but this morning I can't seem to stay away from it.

Like a kindly yet firm owner, I allow my doggy mind to sniff around and try to keep him moving. I'd prevent him from engaging in this low-class sniffing behavior if I could, but we've had that battle for years, and he (my mind) always wins. This morning, using my firmest and not-angry-at-all owner's voice I say, "We're not going to spend ten minutes on each smell, each worrisome thought that comes by." So we explore briefly and keep moving. I notice that it's the same everywhere I look. This morning, everything I encounter is evidence of my deficiency and the impending falling-apart of my life.

But stepping back, even just a little, I admire the brilliance of this mind-state. This anxious mind manifests an unshakable confidence that what it is seeing is the Truth. No soft liberal relativism here. This part of me is sure that he's *exactly right*. And from this confidence, an endless creativity arises: everything that arises is used to bolster the argument. Each new observation is used to further support the perspective that the world is a worrisome place and I am deep in Real Trouble now.

My strategy this morning is just trying not to get totally hooked into one problem—to keep my doggy mind moving. And while I'm still partly asleep, I scan for other ways of working with this worried mind, strategies that might be helpful. I look for images or feelings or dreams that may be lurking in the corner.

In my mind, I come across an image of my hands moving in a way that reminds me of the flow of the flood tide coming up the Medomack River of coastal Maine. While the overall direction is clear and powerful—the tide is irresistibly coming in— the movement of the water in any particular place is chaotic and turbulent. Eddies and microcurrents flow in every direction. Two months ago, I sat in my kayak near the mouth of the river. The tide is full flood and the water beneath my boat seems to be flowing in many directions at once. I imagine that if every current were visible, it would look like an intricate paisley pattern of interlocking curls. Floating in my kayak, I let the gentle currents push me around— spinning the boat and taking me first one direction, then the other.

For some reason, this image, this memory, is comforting to me. Maybe all these worries are just the many currents of my life. Perhaps there is a larger direction that holds it all. What if I trust the deeper flow and just allow the boat of my self to turn with the currents?

I raise my hand to my face and touch my cheek. "There, there," I say to myself. "Everything will be just fine." I'm almost surprised to feel the stubble from my beard. This scared little boy is actually a man who still needs comfort and reassurance on this first morning back in the saddle of his work-life.

And I think of how much I love to ride horses—the power and beauty of their galloping aliveness.

Ah… the trustworthy energy of life, in all its many forms—now I remember.

Parallel Play

Since before my daughter was born in 1986, I've had a pottery studio in our house. When she was just an infant, I used to carry her down to the studio and she would sit on my lap as we played together with the clay. *(First lesson: We don't eat clay.)* Later on, in high school, she learned how to throw pots on the potter's wheel and we worked together on making lots of pots for several pottery sales to support her college expenses. We often sat at our wheels—side-by-side—throwing. She made the bowls and I made the mugs.

Yesterday, we spent the day glazing pots in preparation for two final firings and the dismantling of the studio for our upcoming move. My wife and I are heading to a new home—a sprawling building that we will be making into a Zen Buddhist temple. As my daughter and I mix the glazes and dip our pots, I am very aware that this is almost certainly our last day working together in this studio. Though the new place has room in a huge garage, it is not certain that we will ever set up a clay studio again. This awareness and these thoughts make me unbelievably sad—that kind of sadness that rises like a wave and threatens to crash over me and drag me out to sea.

Even as I struggle to keep going, I am aware that the intensity of these feelings is way out of proportion to the reality of the day. Here I am, spending time with my daughter, doing something we love, and I am lost in this deep grief. As I let myself feel this familiar despair and as I share it with my daughter, I begin to see the deeper sources of the feeling.

The truth is, I don't want anything to change.

Though I love my grown daughter and am delighted with her emerging life and adventures, some other part of me mourns for what is already past. I miss the little girl who played with me for hours—content with the silence of parallel play with clay, with paints, with whatever junk we could glue together. And leaving this house and this studio means coming to terms with the reality that that is truly already over.

So I let myself be with this sadness, the sadness of life—the truth that everything and everyone is constantly slipping through our fingers.

We can't hold on to anything, not even those we most love. Tears and sadness seem to be an appropriate response in the face of the preciousness and transience of our lives. And as I feel and share this feeling, it begins to change—just like everything else in the universe. The wave of intensity recedes. I think of a good glaze combination for the next pot. I hear the singer singing about eyelashes perfectly designed to catch sweat.

And I am here with daughter and myself once again.

The Landscape of Complaint

THE LEG FALLS OFF the plastic side table once again as I lift it up to get myself settled on the back porch this morning. I swear softly—but with feeling. Yesterday's kiln firing is on my mind—too many pots and shelves ruined by bubbling or flaking glazes. I don't even want to look closely. The real estate deal is once again bogged down in complications I only partially understand and the whole project continues to flicker in and out of reality.

I feel defensive and withdrawn, and like I don't want to move—for fear of yet more contact with this world around me that is filled with problems—as if I'm wearing a wet pair of jeans outside on a freezing day.

Everywhere I look is the same bleak landscape and the necessity of another day of carrying a heavy pack with the only destination being somewhere else.

Everything feels like a personal affront.

And yet—a daddy cardinal and his fluffy juvenile son alight on the nearby wire. The trees across the lawn sing with the sound of invisible others. The patient and hardy geranium evenly shares its scarlet greeting with all who come by. Yesterday's tea, reheated, is bitter and warming as I take morning sips.

Perhaps this tightly fisted moment is protective— the circuit-breaker of my soul tripped under the load of too much. Maybe it's OK to be here for a little bit—a respite before reengaging. Here might not be a place of great activity or planning, but it is possibly a place of rest, or of seeing things a different way, or of something yet undiscovered.

Even now, turning toward here, I feel the struggle lessen and some deep clenching subtly ease.

Cars and Waves

We signed the papers yesterday.

My wife Melissa and I begin the process by getting a check from the bank, made out to ourselves, for more money than I ever thought we would have. Then we go to the lawyer's office. Then we give this huge check to the lawyers. Then we sign our names on the same forms over and over. Then we sign more forms. Then they show us the keys to the property but say we can't have them until the papers are submitted to the Grand Authority later this morning. And we all shake hands. I am tempted to spit into my palm first—just to make sure the deal stuck—but I resist.

Afterward, Melissa, who also happens to be a Zen teacher, and I celebrate with two beers and an early dinner. Then we go over to our new property—the one that will be the new Zen center—that will become *Mugendo-ji,* the Boundless Way Temple. We decide to take the law into our own hands and walk around the grounds of this property that is almost, but not yet, ours.

The new house is quite near a main road—Pleasant Street. It's a busy street—especially in the morning and evening as the commuters from the northwest suburbs come in and out of the big city of Worcester. Even though the house is set back and off the road in a way that visually hides it, at 6:00 P.M. when we are walking around, the traffic noise is very noticeable.

I am reminded of the first house Melissa and I bought. When we first walked that property and noticed the traffic noise in the backyard, I was disconsolate. *How could I possibly live with this constant intrusion?* Melissa took my hand and said she thought it sounded like waves on the beach.

In that moment, there in the backyard, I remember thinking I had made the right decision—not just with the house but with this woman of such sweet enthusiasm and imagination. Already I was hearing her Dharma talks—long before she received any formal authorization.

Now, thirty years later, we walk around a much grander house and I wonder if this traffic noise too could sound like waves.

Conscious / Unconscious

THE MYSTIC POET KABIR writes: "Between the conscious and unconscious, the mind has put up a swing: all earth creatures, even the supernovas, sway between these two trees, and it never winds down." This seems about right to me.

Yesterday I led a Zen workshop and miniretreat up in Portland, Maine. There were twelve or thirteen of us, sitting on cushions in a circle—inquiring together into this experience of being human. And in the space between us, in silence and in words, some wisdom arises—not flashy and brilliant, but perhaps more trustworthy than that. We notice firsthand the dependable miracle of the breath and experience the possibility of finding our true home right where we are—in this place, in this moment.

Leading this exploration of being alive always feels to me like a privilege. In that circle, I find words come easily—a knowing appears that I have learned to trust and follow. Sometimes the knowing disappears—and

I am learning to trust and follow even that disappearing. We come together and in the meeting we see each other and are seen. Something happens beyond words.

I leave the day grateful and inspired by our work together.

Driving home, all is well until I pass through the last toll. As I slowly roll through the E-ZPass lane, the green "Thank you!" light fails to come on. I continue through anyway and reach up to check my transponder unit, which is hidden behind the rearview mirror. It's not there.

In an instant, I realize it is in our other car and I have just driven illegally through six tolls in three different states.

I am deeply chagrined. Where has all my wonderful Zen mindfulness and equanimity suddenly gone?

I am now a guilty man, an outlaw. I want to turn myself in and pay the tolls, but I am not sure how to do it. Will they even notice? Will I have to pay big fines for my mindlessness? Will the state police be waiting at my door when I return home? The ruminating mind appears and keeps me company for the rest of my trip.

Swinging between the two trees of conscious and unconscious. So it goes. So *we* go.

And maybe none of it is a problem to be fixed—

just the sea waves of my life running up the inclined beach and falling back only to gather and return once more.

Fear and Faith

IT LOOKS LIKE WE'RE REALLY GOING TO MOVE. The new place is just down the street here in Worcester, but the idea of sorting and packing everything I own fills me with a low-key dread that I don't like at all.

As a good Zen student, I like the idea of simplicity and lack of clutter. In practice, however, I also like all the sweet little things people have given me or I have collected from my travels over the years: the three tiny clay animals a friend gave me for my fiftieth birthday, the pretend bow and arrow I made in a workshop two years ago, the origami sculpture my daughter made when she was fifteen. And then there are the clothes: the t-shirt I painted in 1990 but have never worn, the innumerable pairs of underwear that I stuff in my dresser that occasionally come in handy when I don't have time to do my laundry for several weeks.

What to hold on to? What to let go? As I contemplate these questions I realize that the real issue is the interplay between fear and faith. From the place of fear, I want to hold on to as much as I can—to the memories, to the convenience, to the many options. I see myself in the things around me and begin to "take refuge" in them, to look to them for solace and comfort. To a certain degree, it works.

But from the place of faith, I see that what really sustains me and makes my life possible are not the practical and lovely things of my life, but rather some aliveness and generosity that has no fixed form. So far, every day of my fifty-nine years, I have been given enough to eat. I have found a place to sleep. I have had something to cover my nakedness. And beyond this, most often, I have found myself surrounded with a beauty beyond what I ever dreamed for myself.

The realization of this kind of faith, however, does not yet function freely in my life. Sometimes I see and feel it so clearly, and other times there is a gap, a yawning chasm between this realization and my experience of my life. I expect, to some degree, this will be so all my life. But I also know that my intentions, my thoughts, and my actions have the power to move me toward what is most true and alive or to move me deeper into my fear and clinging.

So my intention today is to practice faith and generosity as I go through my closet letting go of what I no longer need in preparation for what has not yet come.

In the Dark

THIS IS THE FIRST MORNING this season that I'm up in the dark. Even these warm days of early August are growing noticeably shorter. The air hangs heavy under a dim and fuzzy moon. I think maybe I should put the a/c unit back in the window. I remember it's Thursday so I take the bags of trash left over from the retreat out onto the street to be picked up. I pour my freshly brewed hot tea over ice.

I check email and find a beautiful Rilke poem waiting for me, along with some peppy writing from a coaching colleague reminding me that if I'd say no to five more things, my life would be better. But Rilke has already reminded me that I am the bow that shoots the arrow and I am the target—and that feels more true.

I went to my old friend Jack Lund's memorial service yesterday. On the front of the order of service there was a quote from him—his last words to us all who are still here: "Thank you, one and all, for creating me." A wonderful expression of the inter-dependence of our lives. In Buddhism we call this dependent coarising. The self and the world create each other. Our lives are woven together so tightly that when we look closely, we can see that we are not truly separate—not separate from Jack or our parents or our lovers or friends.

Jack was ninety. He was a free-speaker, undeterred by the opinions of others. Always flirting with women and always interested in what you were doing. He was good at saying no and good at saying yes.

Jack was also a sailor—and now he's even more clearly being the wind and the sail, the waves and the boat, as well as captain and crew.

I wish him well as he embarks on this new adventure of death.

View from My New Toilet

SITTING ON MY NEW TOILET in my new bathroom in my new house this morning, I look out the window above my right shoulder toward the first glimmers of morning in the eastern sky. The twinkling morning star above the trees seems a good omen. I call to mind the efforts of my brothers Martin Luther and the Buddha—the former receiving his great revelation on a similar seat and the later upon seeing the morning star—but nothing special happens.

We moved last Saturday. Our flotilla of a twenty-four-foot rental truck, four pickup trucks, and a bevy of assorted cars made three trips along the seven-tenths-of-a-mile path between our two lives—the one we're leaving and the one we're beginning. With the amazing, incredible, and extraordinary assistance of thirty sangha members and friends, we moved the contents of our entire house (and pottery studio) in eight hours.

By four o'clock, everything was in our new house—

in the new Zen center—and we gathered our sweaty bodies to sit together in the zendo for ten minutes of silence. Entering the stillness—spent from the day's emotional and physical efforts—I felt such immense gratitude and exhaustion, I could barely keep from bursting out sobbing. The blessing of this generous community and the potential of what we are creating was palpable.

Now it's Tuesday. Only a few of the boxes have been unpacked, but the meditation hall is neatly arranged with our black square cushions. The Burmese Buddha figure Melissa bought at a tag sale several years ago sits comfortably on his new altar and the statue of the Buddha's mother that a friend loaned us dances on a table in the grand entryway. Here on the new porch I sit in my grandmother's chair and look out through the elegant white columns that frame my new wild backyard.

A stray young maple rises from the bramble on the hillside as if to escape.

Cars rush by on the street behind me.

In this moment, everything is just right.

Measuring Things

I SPEND THE MORNING working on the third floor of the temple with three sangha members. The smallest of us all is four-year-old Riley. He comes to work with his dad and his brand new orange tape measure. The banging of hammers and the excitement of doing important work clearly delights him. Riley seems to understand the deeper totemic meaning embedded in each of the tools. The big socket wrench has special power and is only for his dad. The smaller socket wrench, however, may used by ordinary mortals and is also for children.

Riley's self-appointed job is measuring. He doesn't appear to have a full comprehension of the correspondence of units of length to fixed objects, but he loves to stretch out the endless yellow metal tape and call out the magic incantation of the black numbers. We measure the distance to the wall and across the table and from one random point to another. In the middle of the morning, when the big guys are fully engaged in something or other, Riley calls insistently for our attention. He has carefully stopped the tape five inches out and gleefully announces "It's five! It's five!" as he waves his orange talisman with the thin yellow finger. Clearly there is no need for an outside referent, an object to be measured—the measuring itself is sufficient.

We sometimes talk about the work of Zen as pounding stakes in the clear blue sky or plowing furrows in the sea. These images remind us of the impossibility of measuring this path of being human. The true work of our lives will not hold still to be measured or evaluated in any meaningful way. We come from an infinite distance away and we are on a road to an ever-receding destination—and all of it is right here.

I do believe we can grow in love and understanding, but any attempt to quantify or measure our purported progress is just like stretching Riley's yellow tape from halfway here to halfway there.

"It's five! It's five!"

"I'm alive! I'm alive!"

Kayak Camping

THE AFTERNOON IS HOT AND MUGGY. Dark thunderheads have gathered overhead by the time we reach our launch site in Friendship, Maine. Just as we get our kayaks off the top of the car, we are forced back into the car by driving rain, flashes of lightning, and booming thunder. Perfect timing. An hour later and we would have been on the open water and been executing our lightning emergency drill. (As a licensed Maine Sea Kayak Guide, I explain to my younger sister that this would mean that she holds her paddle vertically while I paddle a safe distance away. But after fifty-nine years of such helpful explanations, she just smiles.)

In fifteen minutes the storm ends as suddenly as it begins, leaving the ocean flat and quiet. We spread out our food, water, camping gear, clothes, and safety equipment next to the kayaks by the water. On every trip at this point, I despair that this necessary pile will fit in the small storage area of our slim kayaks. But somehow, it always does. Just as we finish our packing, the tide agreeably comes under our now heavy boats and with little effort we push out toward the open water.

Once away from shore, our fully loaded kayaks glide almost effortlessly through the mirror-like water. I've been here many times before and feel at home as we paddle along the edge of this working harbor. The many lobster boats rest silently at their moorings. Now posing as a picturesque scene for us paddling tourists, these very same boats will be our diesel alarm clock on the island tomorrow morning as they maneuver between the buoys collecting crustaceans. Our vacationland is their office. But this is Sunday afternoon and all is quiet. The top decks of our long and thin kayaks float mere inches above the flat water and we are the only boats moving.

I love the floating elegance of my kayak. Memories of trips and adventures with friends are present as my paddle rhythmically meets the still water. This ever-changing salt water that covers most of our planet—still dangerously cold if we tip over—now allows us to glide smoothly near the silent rocky shores and tree-covered islands. The clouds clear and the sun carelessly throws its glittering light across the water as we paddle silently together in the beauty of it all.

This evening, with my sister in the boat next to me, I know for sure I am supported by the grace and gravity of this blue-green world.

Invisible Dog

I HAVE DECIDED to get an invisible dog.

I'm tired of being envious of others who go outside and walk the street—not for exercise or anything so virtuous but just because they have to. While I wade through email and plan workshops, they interrupt their important work to walk the dog before he messes the carpet.

So this afternoon I leave my desk and walk slowly down the street in the sweet afternoon sun—just taking the dog out for exercise. I can't go too fast or too far; my imaginary canine friend has to stop and smell everything. For me, an easy saunter, but just breathing the late summer air and feeling the sun on my head seems to be enough.

My invisible dog is old and not very adventurous. Most days he is content just to sniff his way down our familiar street—appreciating the new scents on a well-known tree trunk and noticing the subtle smells of approaching autumn. My dog needs to go out every three or four hours and likes his meals spread out over the course of the day. He's content to lie appreciatively at my feet while I work, but when I stand up, he wants to stretch and be petted. Ah yes, this is what he loves most. He loves attention—to have his ears scratched, to be patted and pushed and played with. He is a great comfort to me, my new invisible dog.

This is our world—the sights and smells, the slow wandering down familiar roads.

Without thinking, we know we belong here.

Unknown Friends

LAST NIGHT I WENT INTO BOSTON to hear a friend give a talk through Harvard Med School. He's a graduate student in immunology and was speaking as part of a series by a student-run organization called "Science in the News." The topic last night was explaining some of how bacteria function in our bodies.

This is what I learned: My body contains more bacteria than the number of people alive on Earth. Though their total mass is only about five pounds, they outnumber the actual cells that I generally consider to be "me." The densest concentration of these microbes is in my large intestine. This is where, I learned, food stays for an average of three days as these microbes work to break down what the rest of my digestive system doesn't. There are so many different microbes that have such interdependent functioning in the large intestine that really really smart people who think about this a lot don't even know all of what is there. Many of these microbes, though essential to my well-being where they are, could kill me if they traveled to other parts of my body.

I'm fascinated by all these parts of me that aren't "me." These microbes are like independent contractors that have their own agenda. I can't order them around and I can't survive without them. On the bright side, I am the whole world to them. But on the down side, I am just a food source, just a place to live. As long as the nutrients keep on coming and I stay away from powerful antibiotics, they are content to go about their microbial way.

So this morning as I take the trash out, I have just a little more respect for the miracle and independence of my colon—"the densest concentration of microbial variety on earth."

And I wonder who should get credit for these thankless household and bodily chores… While I can usually remember Thursday is trash day, I have no clue how I do what I do. Perhaps I'm just a gigantic collaboration of which only a small part is the "me" who thinks he is in charge.

Neurons fire, thoughts arise, and myriad unknown friends and allies work effortlessly in my colon, deep inside the dark mystery I call "me."

AUTUMN

Putting My Self On

I AM LYING IN BED and notice that I'm not asleep anymore. With some focused effort, I open my sticky eyelids to check the clock once more. It's almost 5:00. Nearly time to get up if I want to be able to do some writing before the day's activities begin. I slowly begin to journey back into my life.

Like someone tied up and deposited in an unknown location by his fraternity brothers after a night of wild drinking, I realize that I really don't know where I am. The physical part is the same—I'm in my room in the temple on Pleasant Street—but when I look closely, I notice that each day is radically different. Each day is a new landscape, a new country with new customs and new sights and sounds. And there is a time between sleeping and full waking when I figure out what world I am waking up into. I have to put my self on for the day—like a pair of clothes— selecting the appropriate self for the conditions in which I find myself. I have to look around to take in some information to get a read on where I am. What is the terrain of the world I am in today?

I'm especially aware of this today because yesterday morning was so challenging. I woke to feelings of despair and separation. I hardly remember the content. I just remember that heavy feeling of being stuck in an issue that felt totally unworkable in all its dimensions. This morning is different. I check my body—no major pains or problems—then I imagine forward into my day—an early talk with a Zen student, morning practice at the temple, clients. Then I look into the corners of the day:

Is anything lurking out there to do me harm?

Do I need to be afraid?

Perhaps not—the coast is clear and I notice some lightness through my sleepiness as I shuffle into the bathroom and look out the window into the darkness of the new day.

On the Effort of Falling Leaves

THROUGH THE WINDOW, yellow leaves rain down from invisible branches above. Illuminated by the horizontal sun, each leaf a golden message—a holy text from the universe. In the sure and fluttering descent, each leaf sings a song of praise. Leaf after leaf falls, giving itself to the full embrace of gravity. I marvel at the grand urgency. Each leaf joining perfectly in its appointed time.

This morning I am in love with falling—head over heels falling in love with gravity. Answering the call of the horizontal, I fall from a great height. I am a whole lifetime of falling. I joyfully give myself back to the earth from which I came. Eager to be digested in the belly of all things, I finally surrender to this yearning for return.

There is a beauty in falling—a graceful giving in to the unknowing of my life. But is there even any shred of unknowing in the falling of the leaves? I see nothing tentative or lost in their purposeful activity.

Each is fully supported by all things on its downward journey of grace. Is there any reason to suspect that I am any different? The leaves of the tree and the lilies of the field—and perhaps me too.

Certainly I am equal to a leaf—I am being guided just as surely on my journey, this certain journey of which I know not though it is all I am.

Not Working

THERE IS WORK I AM NOT DOING—bills I should be carefully paying, a desk of clutter to straighten, a stack of books and papers that should be dismantled. But I have escaped to the back porch this late afternoon with the brightly colored pansies smiling at me—purple and white faces that remind me of my grandmother. She would not be happy with this time-wasting.

Like her, I fall naturally into busyness. Not that I intend to—I just find myself carried away with all the good and worthwhile and important things of my life. Periodically (like now) I awaken to realize I am running at full speed with no memory of the acceleration. Traveling pell-mell once again along the familiar roads of responsibility, work, and pressure.

But now I hear children's voices—enthusiastic exclamations, the content of which is lost on the breeze. I imagine these young beings are perfectly innocent in the activity of their play—all going about their business of growing up without the least awareness of any other possibility.

There is work I am gladly not doing.

The breeze pushes bushy treetops that really do look like the green lollipop trees I used to draw.

Under the high blue sky—sitting still I find my way back to the one who knows nothing of work.

Finding a Place

THIS MORNING I wake early looking for a place in the house to feel at home. All my things are here but I'm still wandering—looking for places that belong to me. I already love this nascent temple, which is so alive with the possibilities of community and Zen practice, but I realized last night that I need to find a place to have just for me.

It needs to be like a secret place in the woods—a place you get to only if you know the special paths—the ones that are hidden to the casual observer. You have to remember in your heart how to get there yourself because there are no maps or directions and the terrain keeps changing. And when you get there, you know you are home. The rocks and trees, the ants and birds welcome you back to the secret club of life. In this sanctuary, everything is sacred and significant—from the careful placement of a few sticks on the ground to the prayers that are ceaselessly uttered by the natural arrangement of things. Everything is treasured and you are safe.

In our carefully created living room, I turn the plush golden chair about twenty degrees more toward the window and feel a slight shift. My teacup rests close at hand and my computer is gently warm in my lap. I have only to turn my head slightly to see the black lattice of tree limbs—graceful against the first light of the pale eastern sky. Moonlight comes in the west window.

Maybe this will do.

No Problem, It Just Gets Worse

LIVING IN THE TEMPLE feels like living in a pot that I am making.

This place, both physically and organizationally, is being created as we live here. We are already set up and functioning, and it is also just the beginning. Problems and questions abound. How we will deal with the snow in the parking lot this winter? Should we repair the asphalt around the drain now or wait until the spring? How do we chart a course for the ownership of this place to move from us to the larger organization of our sangha?

Reflecting on this feeling this morning, I recalled a week-long clay workshop I took in the mid-1970s with Bruno LaVerdiere, a former Benedictine monk turned clay artist. In the middle of the week I got stuck with some of the pieces I was working on. The pieces were nearing completion, but I had no idea how to finish and resolve them. I was discouraged and saw no way forward. I went to Bruno to ask for his help in my dilemma and to report my doubts about my capacity to be creative.

Bruno listened patiently to my expression of angst. When I had finished, he laughed and said, "Don't worry, it just gets worse." I was shocked—and reassured. In that moment, the problem, the stuckness, shifted from being what was wrong with me to being part of the creative process itself.

So as the doubts and uncertainties arise, now on a much bigger scale than worrying about how to finish a pot, I turn to this same reassurance. When I move toward the difficulty as part of the process rather than as a comment on me and my capacity, I don't feel stuck in the same way.

Of course I forget, again and again.

And then, of course, I remember.

It keeps getting worse *and* it keeps getting better.

Again and again.

How wonderful!

God Finally Speaks
in a Language I Understand

YESTERDAY, in the middle of an internal tempest—a raging internal debate about my own capacities—I walked to the coffee shop down the road for a treat. On the way, I noticed that the cool air and warm sun seemed perfectly untroubled by the momentous issues and feelings that were swirling through my body.

Nearing the coffee shop, I looked across the street to the mini-mall that has a bead store, a Curves franchise, a beauty salon, and some other shop I can't recall. There, in the window of the salon, was a handwritten sign saying: "Thank you for your devotion."

Now I know there is some logical explanation of why they put that sign in their window that has nothing to do with me. But, in that moment, I knew it was just for me. The universe had decided I needed some direct encouragement to stay the course—to have faith through the turbulence.

I laughed out loud, made a small bow, and got a warm cup of foggy-morning coffee with room for cream.

The Rough Places Plain

This morning, I was inspired to repair a portion of the brick walkway that meanders around the back of the temple. It seems the nearby trees have never fully embraced the river of red bricks. The trees have been waging a slow-motion campaign to disrupt the brick flow by sending out roots under the path. I fancy their eventual aim is to throw the bricks into the air. To date, no bricks have left the ground, but in several sections of the walkway these inert rectangular fellows have been dislodged from their horizontal slumber into small peaks and valleys that threaten to trip the unwary walker.

I chose one small section of disruption and began removing the bricks to uncover the root. My plan was simple—remove bricks, dig out root, cut root, replace dirt, replace bricks. But the ten or twelve bricks I'd imagined removing soon became a pile of twenty or thirty bricks. And then the root turned out to be bigger and had more branches and connections than I had thought. With a shovel, a hand adze, and finally a large axe, I removed the offending section of root. As I worked this underground pruning, I also gave a short lecture to the nearby maple about boundaries and proper function.

She seemed unimpressed—so I offered an apology as well.

After removing this underground cause, I rewarded myself with a cup of freshly brewed coffee in my favorite green plastic camping mug. I stood around for a while just looking at the place where the root used to be—imagining myself one of the guys on the construction crew who leans on a shovel while others work. But since no other work appeared to be done with me resting, I set to work again: replacing the sand bedding, tamping it down, and beginning the process of replacing the bricks.

The pattern was clear—an edging of horizontal bricks and then each interior vertical row offset a half-brick from its neighbors. I began with the edging and proceeded inward. The laying went surprisingly smoothly, the only challenge being to replace the final brick in each row for which there was never quite enough room. But after a few tries, I developed a technique of leaning the final brick and its immediate neighbor against each other in a forty-five-degree angle then pressing them down simultaneously. The force generated pushed each row back just enough to allow the final two bricks to fall into place with a satisfying chunk.

Upon fitting in the last brick and gathering my tools, which had spread over an unnecessarily large area, I stepped back to admire my work. All that was visible was an orderly arrangement of level bricks, but I was filled with an amazing sense of accomplishment and satisfaction. A visceral sense of well-being filled my body and I was taken totally by surprise by the degree of happiness I felt. This repair job was not such a big deal on the grand scale of things, but the orderly pleasure of the patterned bricks—the possibility of making "the rough places plain," the physicality of it all—touched me deeply.

I do love this carnal world—these miraculous bodies that bend and lift and touch. I love the patterns and possibilities we can create. We can make paths and gardens and dinners and music. We can repair what is broken. We can create shapes and spaces that have the power to delight—to touch our souls in the place before words.

And one very small corner of the world is now more orderly and beautiful than it was before.

Falling For Good

HERE IN NEW ENGLAND, the days have grown quite short now. And just the other day we had our first wet snow of the season. The nasturtiums that grew riotously over the slope behind the pergola now lie flat—victims of the hard frost a couple days ago. The marigolds too, once bushy and covered with flashy orange blossoms, are brown and wilted. Only the carcasses of tomato plants still stand erect. The stakes and cages that once kindly held the weight of their fruit are now superfluous and seem almost cruel.

Only the giant beech tree by the road seems to have missed earth's seasonal memo on the timeliness of letting go. She stubbornly grips her green leaves, even while her partner, the majestic oak, has dropped his leaves at her feet. She studiously ignores his entreaties and holds fast to her own sense of things.

But even for her, it won't be long.

This fall, though I have continued to love the endless falling of the leaves, I have been thinking more about the finality of the activity. Of course it's part of the cycle and I know these same trees will sprout new and amazing leaves in the spring. But for the leaves that fall, this leaf identity, this leaf-life, is really over. They won't jump up in the spring and say, "Just kidding!" and find their way back to the branches from which they fell. They're not migrating birds who miraculously find their way back to their birth place.

In the midst of the cycle of the seasons—of light and dark, of life and death—there is also this one-way movement. The job of the fallen leaves is not to rise up but to fall further apart—until there is nothing leaf-like that remains. I rake them onto tarps and drag them ceremoniously to the six-foot pile by the back fence to await their dissolution. Some day in the spring, several years from now, I will spread the rich humus of their remains back over the garden.

Or perhaps someone else will be doing that work by then.

This dying business is not merely poetic. It feels important this morning to find my way into both the closing of the season that only precedes next spring's opening, as well as into that which is fully lost—the parts and pieces of life that only throw themselves forward into the future through completely dissolving.

I know that I too, in the midst of the cycles of the days and the seasons of my life, am slowly being called toward this dissolution.

Recovery

I CAN ALMOST LAUGH AGAIN NOW.

I still have to grab for a pillow to hold to my belly, but I'm off pain medication and "resting comfortably." Not so the past five days.

Tuesday, I was operated on. I'm now quite clear it was not simply an "abdominal procedure"—as my doctor had called it—but a full-on operation. I have a lovely row of metal staples in my belly to prove it. I'm told the cutting and repairing and stapling back up all went quite well.

I remember being wheeled into a large room with big lights, being asked to put on a mask and take a few deep breaths. The next thing I was aware of were the voices of the nurses in the recovery room—then the welcomed faces of my wife and daughter in the resting room. Thirty minutes later I put my clothes on, stood up to sit in the wheel chair, was wheeled to the car, and driven home.

These last five days have been better and worse

than I imagined. I've been practicing prayer, meditation, and letting go. My success, as usual, has been partial. I can't deny moments of luxurious ease—almost floating on my bed, medication working, and no desire to read or write or talk—just being here. I have also felt quite loved and cared for by my wife and the few friends I have asked for help. They all seem to have this affection for me that is unrelated to my "functioning well." Here I am, laying helplessly in bed—not solving problems, not listening attentively, not contributing to the common good in any way I can discern—and still people seem to like me and want to help me.

This is quite puzzling to me and I am determined, at some point, to figure out how this could be possible.

And what a challenge to be in the land of undependable body, intermittent pain, and wanting it to be different. I suppose this is the land of being human, but it all gets quite vivid at times like this. Theory and good ideas are of little use in the immediacy of pain and the fear of more to come. But even here, where there is no escape, the practice of being in the moment has been at least a direction.

Also a glimmer that even in the worst pain and stuckness, this too might be it.

Letting Go

THE UNSAVORY AND MIRACULOUS daily activity of the bowels is an intricately choreographed dance of contraction and release that most of us would just as soon not think about.

But when the dance stops, few things take center stage so insistently and urgently.

After the surgery, my whole abdomen seemed shut down. That whole region was pain and I seemed to want my attention anywhere but there. I ate to get strength back, not out of hunger. Peeing was the first hurdle—that came on the first day—but it wasn't till the third day that I got rumblings of something more wanting to come out. The incision was still quite painful and I couldn't sit long on the toilet without discomfort. And I was afraid letting go would hurt— so I was in a perfect double bind—couldn't hold on and couldn't let go.

Numerous trips to the toilet resulted in no output and greater discouragement. I felt like a little boy whose father is trying to toilet train him when he has no interest in cooperating. As the little boy, I dutifully go in to the toilet, assume the seated position, and wait for some miraculous production. But nothing happens. With each unsuccessful attempt, my internal father becomes more agitated. I began to truly despair that this prosaic act of release would ever happen again. I had visions of being taken to the emergency room in total shame and embarrassment.

So I have been sitting on the toilet—desperately wanting to let it out, to release. Yet equally strong is the elemental urge to hold it in. I am afraid of the pain—afraid of what is to come. Straining as I clutch a pillow to my belly to support my incision—I am perfectly stuck.

And from this place of no escape I am also calling out to all the buddhas and bodhisattvas, calling out to God, to be rescued. And in the midst of it all, considering the possibility that even this straining of impossibility is the life of all worlds. This is perfectly OK. Right here. Even this.

This place of stuck—"I have to" and "I can't"—feels familiar from my spiritual work. We're told to simply "let go"—but when we try to do this, we often seem to get more deeply tangled in the willful web of resistance. In spite of injunctions to the contrary, "letting go" doesn't appear to be something we have conscious control over. Why can't we just let go into the loving arms of the universe? What is this holding back that seems so essential—so imperative?

I encounter this vital resistance again and again when I sit in Zen meditation. I have spent long hours in the meditation hall with a running dialogue of internal complaint. *My back hurts. I'm bored. Why can't I do this right? Why can't I just accept where I am?* I long to let go—to be released from my self-imposed isolation. And yet I resist. Why is this so? This holding back—such a mystery. And when I fight it, it just gets worse. Fighting seems to give it more power.

Eventually, the release did happen. The necessity of nature overcame the pattern of resistance known as David, and my bowels moved. This was indeed a blessed event and has given me a new appreciation for this daily spiritual practice of letting go of what is no longer necessary—and also for this *stuck* place, this place where we can't go forward and we can't go back.

Release seems to come only when we allow ourselves to be truly stuck—when we find ourselves all out of tricks and skillful means.

As we allow ourselves to surrender to the prosaic and the holy in the particular form of this moment,

we open ourselves to the grace of letting things be—
the grace that functions effortlessly and is, indeed,
the very fabric of our life.

Practicing Love

IN COLLEGE in the early '70s, someone told me you should practice loving by starting out with a rock.

I took him seriously and for a while carried a rock with me at all times. It was a big enough rock that it wouldn't fit in my pocket, so it was a great conversation starter—like a pet, only weirder. From my perspective, the rock and I had a pretty good relationship. I was devoted and respectful. The rock accepted me exactly as I was and was totally dependable.

I can't remember how it ended. I imagine the passion faded and we just parted ways.

Several years after that, Melissa and I moved in together—into a small apartment near the Wesleyan University campus. Our "bedroom" was more like a closet, just big enough for the thin futon that we unrolled on the floor. The first night I realized our backyard was adjacent to the air conditioning system for a university building that rumbled and rattled that whole hot summer night. I was sure we had made a huge mistake.

It was on that day, in the afternoon, I brought home a kitten. Held in one hand behind my back, a gray ball of fur, this irresistible cuteness—a present for this irresistible woman who had turned my life upside down. We called the kitten Mullein, after the gray-green fuzzy herb, and we thought we would practice being parents with her. She was always slightly crazy and would dash wildly at random intervals from one end of the apartment, or house, to the other. We often wondered if this was a reflection on our capacity as parents.

We were brokenhearted when Mullein died in Melissa's arms some ten years later.

Our daughter, Rachel—who was three or four at the time and was already turning out much better than the cat—was brokenhearted too.

I still like the idea of practicing loving by beginning with what is around us—the rocks and trees, the desks and sinks, the dogs and cats.

Other human beings, especially ones we really care about, are so complicated and challenging that we would do well to get all the practice we can.

Breakfast at the Temple

In our backyard, behind the temple and not visible from the road, are two crab apple trees. When the leaves fell this autumn, the red cherry-like fruit was revealed. With these two extravagant bird feeders, we've been a popular culinary destination for birds of all sorts.

Even the littlest birds seem to swallow the fruit whole as they gorge in preparation for the cold to come.

Yesterday morning it was especially crowded and delightfully noisy. As we settled down to our morning meditation practice, the birds were already chanting. From the general tone and joy of the sound, I suspect they were reciting the many names of buddhas and bodhisattvas—though it was hard to make out their precise meaning.

A few hours later, a much larger bird landed on a branch just beyond the fruit trees. He perched obligingly while I grabbed my binoculars for a better look. An impressive sight, he must have been a foot tall with a prominent white breast streaked with brownish flecks. After a few moments he flew to the ground, revealing the distinctive reddish coloring on the underside of his tail: a red-tailed hawk—come for breakfast too. It wasn't the ripe red fruit he was after but rather the tender morsels of feathers and flesh.

He may have been too late—the former singing patrons had fled and it was silent. I was glad for the apparent escape of the little chirping ones.

But some wilder aspect of me was strangely restless and unsatisfied.

While we usually root for the fuzzy parts of nature with the large eyes, we are just as much dependent on the seeming cruelty of the predators.

All is present and all is necessary in this intricately choreographed dance we call life.

Growing Up Together

My mother's tests came back negative—in the good way.

There's nothing wrong with her. She's a healthy eighty-year-old woman. She used to be so young— though I never suspected it at the time. I have grown up with her and now I see that she has grown up with me.

We grow up together—parents and children equally. We all teach each other and learn from each other as best we can. The specific roles—so defining and powerful in the beginning—tend to loosen and shift with the many years. Caretaking shifts from being one-way to mutual—and then often becomes one-way in the other direction.

Dependence swings back and forth.

We care for each other as best we can.

If we are very lucky, we grow old together.

I love how unconscious we are as children. We hardly know our parents are taking care of us. We are just living our lives. Our lives are so obvious we rarely see the precarious balance—the precious give and take of each moment.

Now grown-up and growing old myself, I suspect we are still unconscious on some level—still imagining that we are taking care of ourselves—rarely appreciating the fantastic web of dependence and support that sustains us as we go about our serious play of being human.

No Such Thing as a Zen Master

MY TRANSMISSION IS COMING.

Not the kind you put in your car but the Zen kind, Dharma Transmission—the formal recognition from teacher to student of the completion of training. My teacher, George Bowman, is also called Zen Master Bomun. Zen Master Bomun received this transmission from his teacher, the great popularizer of Korean Zen, Zen Master Seung Sahn, who in turn received it from his teacher, and so on back to the Buddha—at least according to myth and story. Now it is my turn.

This is a real problem for me.

I've been studying and training with George for twenty years—countless days on silent retreats, innumerable conversations and questions. Through our work together, I have encountered something of unsurpassable value—something I have found to be utterly dependable and infinitely resourceful. In

Buddhism, we call it the Dharma, but it could just as easily be called the Tao or God or the Source of All Things or Rama-Lama-Ding-Dong.

And yet whatever we call it or imagine it to be, it is essentially ungraspable and cannot be contained. As Bodhidharma said, it is "beyond words and letters."

This is where the problem lies.

If it is ungraspable and beyond conception, how can anyone be so presumptuous as to claim to have "completed" their study of this great matter, let alone to be a "Master" of it? Yet in the Zen tradition, this ineffable something has been passed down from teacher to student for twenty-five hundred years. The women and men who have passed it on are sometimes called "Zen Master," sometimes "Roshi"—but just as often, "Hey you."

The transmission ceremony will happen in the spring. Honored and humbled—excited and terrified—I am inspired to continue and deepen my Zen journey.

Fortunately for me, there is no end to this training, and there has never been any such thing as a Zen Master.

A Day Off?

THIS EARLY SUNDAY morning sky is dark and clear after last night's unexpectedly early snow. The predicted six-to-ten inches turns out to be only one or two—but all of that sticking to the colder branches as it fell. Now the sky brightens and the confused horizon of rooftops and trees begins to color.

Me—sitting here by the window in the warm house. Cars occasionally going by in front. Now the sound of a snow shovel across the street—scraping against the frozen snow. The top orange edge of the sun shows itself through the white branches to the southeast. I'm briefly blinded as I foolishly look directly at it.

There's no stopping this day now. Even this pale winter sun fills the white world.

Surprisingly, I have no particular plans for what to do while the sun describes its shallow winter arc of today. Of course, much should be done, but the morning is young and my head still slow with sleep.

I wander freely, here in my morning chair, in a world of possibility. The responsible person I usually am waits patiently by—like a set of formal clothes laid out for the day. But for now, just these comfortable and barely presentable sweat pants.

I know there are ways to follow rather than lead— ways to be surprised even in the small things.

Maybe I'll trust the world to function today without my guidance.

Maybe I'll take the day off and let the clothes of my usual self rest gently on the bed.

This Sweet Little Hum

I'M JUST BACK from a three-day Zen meditation retreat. After these many years of practice and countless retreats, I am still amazed at what unfolds in this brief time.

Sitting quietly with other human beings—walking together, eating together—we enter a wilder and more vivid realm of living.

Sitting still, I see that the world is not a solid thing outside me, but rather some kind of process—continually shape-shifting with me and through me. The ease of one moment vanishes and confusion reigns. Then confusion gives way and something else appears.

Each day, each sitting period, each breath is a whole lifetime. The ten thousand joys and sorrows make their appearances and each is the fullness of human life.

Each step is the destination.

But amid all the coming and going, there is something else. A friend once called it "this sweet little hum." This hum of aliveness. This song of the universe. This vibration of life.

You can sing it, but you can't name it. You can live it, but you can't have it.

What is the hum of your life? What is there that doesn't come and go?

Getting still again I listen and wonder.

In Zen practice, we especially value the wondering—the intentional wandering that leads us to an intimacy beyond our conception. In the field of this moment we can learn to hear and sing along.

And perhaps, if the silence is deep and the timing just right, we can be the hum itself.

Unintended Consequences

ONCE ON A TRAIN IN NORTHERN WALES, Melissa and I met a British professor of American History. He told us of a book he had just written about the unintended consequences of American wars. His thesis was that the major consequences of every war were unplanned and unforeseen at the outset. The intentions of the participants turned out to have only a small correlation to the actual results of their actions.

I suspect this applies to all human endeavors.

We begin with some image or vision of what we want, but as we move into the thing itself, our original impulse is changed in some way.

I'm thinking of this because our decision to install a fire suppression sprinkler system in the basement dormitory of the temple has led to the strong likelihood of purchasing a two-ton Buddha statue.

And the necessity to construct a handicap access ramp at the front of the temple may have provided the perfect courtyard for this seated Buddha.

It all began in a casual conversation with John, the owner of the paving and excavating company. We hired them to tear up our parking lot to bring in a new water line from the street. John told me that a friend of his was trying to "unload" a large Buddha statue. Apparently the customer who ordered it, upon seeing it in person, realized the piece was far too big for his lawn. That gentleman has since ordered a Buddha figure half this size. The company, or the customer, I'm not sure which, was stuck with a five-foot carved granite Buddha that they were willing to sell for "short money." John said he thought it might be perfect for us here at the temple.

That afternoon I called the number he gave me and was told they did indeed have such a Buddha, but they had already offered it to one of the other Buddhist temples in town. I suspected that would be the end of the story—but I got a call the next day informing me that the other temple had just paved their parking lot and didn't want a large truck with a heavy statue driving over the new pavement.

I got directions to the storage lot and permission for a visitation. I found the Buddha sitting behind three running horses and beside a naked woman lying languidly in a hammock. Even in the midst of such tantalizing distractions he sat motionless—as were, I must admit, the stone horses and the white marble woman. But I was most amazed at his size. A five-foot statue doesn't sound large until you factor in the seated pose and the presence of that much stone. I suspect that if this Buddha figure stood up, he would be around nine feet tall. I later found out that he weighs in at a svelte four thousand pounds.

I returned with photos and a sense that he was probably too big for us. This was not a charming little Buddha statue to tuck away in some unexpected corner of the property. This was a centerpiece, a focus of attention in almost any location. When I reported back to my colleagues James and Melissa, they were both immediately in favor of purchasing this Buddha. We thought about it, then called back, negotiated a price of $1,500, and made the commitment to purchase the statue. They said they would deliver it (with boom crane truck) for free.

We don't yet know where the money will come from, but I'm sending a deposit in today.

So this is how obeying city fire safety codes can lead to a five-foot Buddha statue outside your front door.

Be careful.

Just Drinking Coffee

YESTERDAY MORNING, I used the birthday money my mother sent me to buy a pottery mug at the Worcester Center for Crafts annual holiday sale.

The mug is amazingly beautiful and cost an unreasonable amount. The marks of flame and ash from its wood-fired origins are the natural decoration on this smallish drinking vessel. The cup itself was pushed in as the handle was attached, so the sweet memory of soft wet clay lingers with the finished piece. The handle itself is elegant, chunky, and reliable.

I paid a wild forty dollars for the mug and probably wouldn't have done it with "my own" money. But as a birthday extravagance, I could justify the purchase. Having been a professional potter many years ago, I suspect that the maker of my mug works long days, both in the making and in the selling of his creations. And if his annual net is thirty thousand a year, I'm sure he considers himself quite successful.

Later in the day, I went to my local Ace Hardware

store to buy a replacement halogen bulb for one of the space-age light fixtures that fly from the temple's kitchen ceiling. Ace is the chain store that drove out of business the previous, locally owned hardware store with wooden floors and guys who knew how to fix things. They often have great bargains at Ace because now they are hanging on for their economic life due to the Home Depot that opened a few miles away.

On the way out, in the center aisle, which is the seasonal bargain display, I saw a four-cup coffee maker along with the snow shovels and window scrapers. I have been half-heartedly looking for a small coffee-maker ever since I gave away our old one to my father last Father's Day when he was passing through town on an RV camping trip and had forgotten his coffee-maker. So I checked the price on the coffee-maker, and when I saw it was an amazing nine dollars, I scooped one up—along with my tiny don't-touch with-your-fingers, seven-dollar halogen bulb.

Later this morning, I will go into the kitchen, turn on my seven-dollar light bulb, brew some ten-dollar-a-pound dark-roast coffee in my nine-dollar coffee-maker, and then drink a small cup of joe in my forty-dollar mug.

This all makes me conscious of the invisible webs of relationships I support as I live my economic life.

I know the name of the man who made the mug. He lives in Maine and I am happy to share some of the money that people give me with him. The people who made the parts and assembled the coffee-maker and packed it and put it on the trucks and put it in the center aisle of Ace Hardware are more hidden from my imagination—I suspect most of them, like the potter, would be happy to make so princely a sum as the equivalent of thirty thousand a year.

I feel virtuous about supporting the potter (even though it was my mother's money)—and while I am happy to get such a great deal on my new coffee-maker, I feel vaguely uneasy about the way the frugality I foster in some parts of my life is not unrelated to the poverty that persists elsewhere.

Buddha Comes to Boundless Way Temple

OF COURSE buddha—our awakened nature—has long been here, but Buddha, the beautiful two-ton granite statue, arrived at the temple yesterday morning. Seeing him prominently sitting on the back of the flatbed truck filled me with delight. He sat in perfect zazen posture with blue moving blankets keeping his stone legs warm and yellow straps like a seatbelt holding him firmly in place.

This new Buddha figure is a landmark. Our temple (and home), which used to look like a large white New England house with a very attractive handicap access ramp, is now visibly aligned with this ancient tradition of Buddhism. Our collective vision of this house and these grounds as a center for Zen practice, retreats, and training is now manifest—not just in the daily practice schedule and the training retreats we have held, but in this large statue that now sits by the front door.

This statue is also a demonstration of the way the universe responds when we clearly set out in some direction.

I don't believe the universe has a personality or does really "respond" in a way we can understand, but I have seen amazing things happen when we clarify our intention. Maybe it's just that we notice different things that were there all along. Maybe it's that we tell a different story about the same things that would have happened anyway. Whatever the reason, I regularly see unexpected and beneficial things arise in support of those individuals or see groups clarify a vision that deeply touches them.

By all reasonable laws of nature, this statue shouldn't be here. We weren't looking for it. We didn't have the extra money to spend on something that was not essential. And we have many other projects and needs going on. Yet someone mentioned it, I followed up, got encouragement at just the right time, and a number of people have started contributing money to make this all possible.

The statue itself is unreasonably beautiful.

I suppose, like a proud parent, I am already biased, but I have seen many Buddha statues and this one has something special. At five feet tall seated, the monumental scale alone gives it a powerful presence. But it's more the face. In the lowered eyes and gentle

expression, the sculptors in China (who carve buddhas for temples all over Asia) have caught something
of the serenity and spaciousness of Zen.

The crane on the back of the delivery truck could
barely manage the weight of the statue, so they lifted
him and swung him around in stages. Several of us
were there to witness this flying two-ton Buddha as
he completed the final stages of his journey toward
us. We made sure he was centered in front of the
weeping cherry tree—on the level bed of gravel that
had been carefully raked in preparation—and then he
was lowered. We chanted the "Sho Sai Myo Kichijo
Dharani" (a chant whose mysterious power averts
disasters) while he was being lifted and later offered
incense to welcome him.

It's not the statue that's important, but rather
this physical manifestation of some aliveness that is
totally beyond form.

This ungraspable source has been passed down
to us in the tradition of Zen Buddhism through the
efforts of countless men and women through the
centuries.

Though there are many ways to honor and move
toward this aliveness—for me, and for the followers
of the Zen path, the simple practice of sitting still
and being present with our lives is a gift beyond measure. Something not just to read, or to hope happens,

but each time we sit in meditation it is something we manifest. We participate in the mystery itself.

This is the gift of this particular tradition that we have chosen—that has chosen us.

We welcome this new hunk of granite that will sit outside our front door as a reminder of our vows, our vision, and this rich tradition of Buddhism.

WINTER

Wanting to Be William

I WOKE UP this morning wishing I were William James.

I went to sleep last night in the middle of his essay "The Will to Believe." Reading his dense and brilliant prose I feel the force of his mind—I underline the really good stuff and struggle to keep my own mind loose enough to follow his closely reasoned argument. The last thing I saw before my head hit the pillow was his bearded portrait on the black cover of his collected essays. Looking straight ahead, he is the embodiment of *gravitas*.

Looking right at me, he doesn't blink as I gently lay him down on the floor by my bed, turn out the light, and close my eyes.

I distinctly remember wanting to be my father when I was little. He was the minister up in front of all the people who sat politely listening and then shook his hand at the church door when they left. I would stand next to him holding his other hand as he said goodbye to everyone. They all seemed to know my name and I knew to smile and say hello without knowing theirs.

I saw clearly that my father was the center of some bright universe, that he was clearly everything a man should be.

Of course I grew up to see more clearly his strengths and weaknesses—his gifts and blindnesses. Like the rest of us, he had no choice but to be himself as best he could. He had to uncover and use his gifts. He had to work with the deep loneliness and desperation that he inherited from his mother and father and their mothers and fathers.

I too have inherited this fierce need to connect and the sometimes crippling sense of never being enough.

But I think I was nearer the truth as a young boy pulling on my dark-robed and smiling daddy's hand by the door of the church. He was (and is) brilliant and admirable—standing as every person stands, at the center of his or her only possible universe. His gifts came out of his weaknesses and nothing could save him, or me, from our great discouragements and failures.

And William James—he too had his life to live, both heroic and petty. I know from his own writing that neither his many gifts nor the admiration of his peers and posterity saved him from the fullness and suffering of his human life.

I suppose I will have to continue to learn to take myself as I am, to hold out the unreasonable hope that just this life, just being David, is enough—and perhaps more than enough.

Christmas Practice

YESTERDAY, thoughts of my family and friends kept going through my head.

I suppose this could be a good thing, but in my case, the thoughts were mostly worrying about what I should get them for Christmas.

Not coming up with many good ideas, I began to feel increasingly uncomfortable and inadequate. Reflecting on it this morning, I notice how easily this inescapable holiday of giving gifts turns into an experience of personal inadequacy. I love these people and it gives me joy to make them happy—but this appreciation and aspiration quickly becomes responsibility and burden (*I'd better get the* RIGHT *presents and I don't know when I'm going to do it*).

And it's not just Christmas.

I often start with a good intention, but then the intention becomes a "task" and becomes disconnected from the original purpose. Some urge comes from my heart, but reaching the light of day, it gets written down on my to-do list and becomes just one more thing I have to accomplish—one more way I have to measure up.

Even my deepest wishes for my life transform into just one more thing on my never-ending list. My daily meditation easily becomes an exercise in self-discipline rather than an expression of my love. The writing that I find so nourishing becomes an impossible task that I must once again turn to face.

Noticing this universal tendency for things to split apart, I remember (again) that my most important work is remembering my deeper intention. In the midst of the busyness of all the doing, I need to regularly turn toward the underlying heart connection that is the source.

In this case, I go back to my purpose in giving gifts to family and friends. What is all this really about?

So today, as I spend time figuring out what presents to give, I vow to keep going back to the love and wish for joy that I have for family and friends. And as the feelings of obligation and unease arise, may they be a reminder to turn yet again to something deeper and more dependable.

This is my practice for today.

Receiving and Giving

THIS DARK DECEMBER MORNING, I sit in my comfortable writing chair next to the radiator with a cup of tea and a blanket. My white laptop warms my lap top, and my green bought-in-Oregon hat covers my bald head top. The radiator hisses for a few moments, then begins its soft expansive pinging. I feel the faint sense of warmth on my cheek. My fingers do their exquisite tap dance on the keyboard. I don't really know how they do it, and I appreciate their functional wisdom, which is not owned by the person I imagine myself to be.

Lots of snow is forecast for today and in this moment, I'm grateful to the generosity of the radiator—its willingness to serve through receiving and giving, living its one true life of expansion and contraction. I hear the furnace click on and the whoosh of the burner. Then the hissing as the cold radiator receives the hot steam from the boiler below. Next the pinging begins—always the random rhythm for just a few moments. I like to imagine the sleepy radiator electrons waking up. Thrilled by the heat of the water vapor, they begin their eager buzzing. And in this waking up, in this symphonic humming of life—ever so slightly, the whole radiator enlarges, as if it were breathing in.

The excitement travels quickly to the radiator surface and passes into the air. Through the air to my cheek and eventually all the way across the room to the thermostat—expanding the metal coil to break the connection and stop the furnace.

Even as I sit writing, this cycle happens several times. Someday we should replace these old drafty windows—this old New England house costs a fortune to heat.

But for this morning, I appreciate the receiving and the giving that is the life of my radiator and my life too.

Trusting the Aliveness

I SEEM TO BE FINDING MY WAY by losing it, particularly in writing. I notice that there is a way of writing that seems to squeeze the life out of me. The deep and persistent urge I have to write a book becomes an external goal or standard I have to live up to. The shift itself is quite subtle and I cross over the line from aliveness to "hard work" without noticing.

My tendency, in moments of difficulty, is to bear down and work harder.

This works quite well in some areas, but our true path cannot be uncovered or walked through an act of will. Of course there has to be effort—without clear intention we simply wander in the trance of everyday life. But our effort has to be an opening to something greater—an expression of something already here rather than a striving for something we imagine is in the distance.

Or at least this is the way it is for me.

I can't seem to write a book that lays out a clear

framework for how we should live our lives. I've got a framework in my mind, but every time I try to write about it, I slip out of my experience and into my head. The words I write on the page make sense, and perhaps may even be good advice, but I get bored writing them. My attention wanders and internally I have to play the part of the strict schoolteacher who tells the unruly class to stop looking out the window—to stop passing notes and get back to reading about Dick and Jane.

What I really want is to let the class run wild and see what happens.

I want to trust the aliveness of the moment and be able to follow the unfolding long enough to come to some new place. I don't want to write about what I know; I want to write about what I don't know— about the passionate and beating heart of things that takes no fixed form.

What is the form that will contain all this?

The Spirit of Receiving

OF ALL THE CHRISTMAS GIFTS I have ever received, one of my most favorite was from my two younger sisters, Ellen and Janet. They were four and three years old. I was a lordly nine.

We lived at Thirty-Seven-Oh-Five Frazier Road in Endwell, New York, the front yard of which was the scene of many touch football games with my father, brother, and the neighborhood kids. You had to be careful how you utilized the talents of the younger players—the three-year-olds were notoriously poor on catching the long passes.

It was the year Ellen and Janet realized that not only did people get gifts on Christmas, they *gave* gifts too. Being short on cash at that point in their lives and wanting to give something to their older brothers, they decided to give something they owned. They found three or four stray books that they no longer liked, wrapped them together, and put them under the Christmas tree.

I vividly remember their excitement and pride that Christmas morning as they jointly presented this clumsily wrapped package to me and my brother Steve. In retrospect, I suspect my mother may have given us a warning or coached us a little on the importance of accepting this gift. But, whatever the preparation, I remember my two dear sisters, full of joy and love, giving me this very special gift. And opening the package and finding their old books, I was truly delighted. And though it was clear they had yet to master the subtleties of the art of giving (I now suspect this is true for all of us), they did their best and had chosen me and my brother to receive the gift of their love.

Later today, as I celebrate Christmas giving with my wife, adult daughter, and close family friends, I hope to receive the heart of every gift with the same joy and honor I experienced from that gift so many years ago.

New Year's Wishes

BUDDHA IS UP TO HIS NECK in snow but doesn't seem to mind.

He just sits there, still smiling under the weeping cherry tree.

I like to imagine he's smiling because the spring blossoms are already dancing in his head. Or better yet, that the bare winter branches are already beauty enough for him.

I myself seem to be hard-wired for impatience. Once at a workshop, the instruction was to walk mindfully over to the lunchtime food across the room. In that short walk across the room, I noticed how automatically I get ahead of myself—how I lose track of these miraculous feet on the ground and miss the space in between. And I'm beginning to suspect that most of life is "in between."

So my New Year's wish this morning is to appreciate my feet on the floor and the vast space of all the moments in between.

And as long as I'm wishing, I'd like to wish for a new appreciation of my impatience as well—that I might see impatience like the dark lines of the winter weeping cherry branches behind the Buddha—beautiful for what they are, not just for what they will be.

Most Important Is Patience

LAST WEEKEND I had the opportunity to work with an inspiring group of teachers from an inner-city charter school in Memphis. Their commitment to keep their eyes and hearts open in the face of the suffering they see daily was palpable. As they talked about the qualities and values they wanted to impart to their students, the one that caught me off-guard was the value of patience.

It was the math teacher who observed that patience—the ability to stay with a problem that doesn't yield to an easy solution—is the primary skill necessary for doing well in his subject. Without the capacity to stay with the discomfort of not yet knowing, there is no opportunity to come to new learning. The job of the student is to hold his or her attention on the subject at hand until the brain is able to make the new connections necessary to solve this new problem. It's just a matter of time.

As I consider this perspective, the truth and the

practical value of patience feels quite vivid to me in almost every area of my life—from my work of writing, to my meditation practice, to my ongoing relationships. Like an impatient teenager, I often want to have immediate results. When success or completion doesn't come quickly, my urge is to blame myself ("I can't do this!") or circumstances ("This is too hard!") or to run away ("I don't care about this anyway!").

But seeing patience as the primary skill, the problem of the day or of this period of my life becomes just the place I am rather than the next measurement of my worth as a human being. And from this perspective I can more easily let this mysterious brain (and heart) make the necessary connections.

My job is just to stay present with as much openness and curiosity as I can manage.

Bird Watching

THE FROZEN SNOW outside my kitchen window reflects the harsh morning brightness. Three gray squirrels scamper nervously under the dangling birdfeeder, quivering as they eat the scattered seed that has fallen from above. I don't begrudge them the seed on the ground. But yesterday, one of these scruffy fellows summitted the feeder pole to go after the hanging suet.

He easily climbed the smooth metal pole to right below the squirrel-proof inverted cone that blocked his path. Then, reaching out with one amazing paw, he grabbed the granular snow on the topside of the cone, swung out, and in one frantic brilliant scramble, reached the pole and then the sweet suet. While I admired his performance, I was also offended.

Determined to defend my intended offering to the birds, I gathered the slingshot and hazelnut ammunition that a friend had given me for just such an eventuality. Stealthily opening the kitchen window to the frigid air, I zinged one dangerous nut just past his surprised left shoulder. He lightly leapt down and seemed to smile slightly as he and his friends bounded away.

I suspect he will continue to have the better of me—what with his having more time to experiment and with the necessity of eating as his motivation, as opposed to my general sense that I want to make an offering to the birds rather than to the squirrels.

But, for the time being, I am committed to my objection, and I plan to keep my slingshot and my hazelnuts close at hand.

Termination Papers

A FRIEND OF MINE had to go in to work to sign his termination papers last week. He had been on a three-month health leave due to symptoms from his progressing multiple sclerosis.

The plan of the leave had been to regain his strength, but it didn't work.

So on Tuesday, he went in to sign out of the work force.

I had breakfast with him on Thursday. He was still in shock—not just at having lost his job, but dealing with the idea that he will mostly likely never work again. And here was his retirement party—a couple of guys in a diner eating fried eggs and drinking coffee.

No gold watch, no celebrating achievements, just an offer of continued health coverage—if you're able to pay for it yourself.

We did our best to honor this fearsome marking point. It's not going to get better: best-case scenario is that his physical diminishment happens slowly.

Being with him, I was conscious that this task—the difficult task of losing what we have—is the work ahead for all of us. The journey of being human inexorably leads to the loss of all bodily function—a state commonly called death.

And though there are varying opinions about the landscape beyond, it seems quite clear that we don't get to take much with us. Not our treasured knick-knacks. Not our achievements. Not the people who are most precious to us. We can't even take this most intimate body of flesh. It appears that everything has to be left at the door. We must enter helpless—relying on some power beyond our knowing to sustain and guide us.

So this morning I say a prayer for my friend and for all those that are struggling with sickness, illness, and diminished capacities.

I also say this prayer for those of us who are still in the midst of activity and the appearance of ascendancy and accumulation.

The prayer is that we might learn to trust more deeply the source from which everything arises and everything returns, the source that has sustained us from our first breath.

And that in this vast inconceivable source, we might find comfort and ease as we join without regret into the rising and falling of all things.

Knowing Where to Go

THE INSIDE OF the New England Aquarium is dark and filled with parents and children this cold Saturday afternoon.

Everywhere I look, I see manifestations of limitless creativity—the brilliantly colored, oddly shaped fish, the elegant and gossamer jellyfish, the awkward hopping penguins that fly through the water as if it were thin air.

But I want to tell you about the baby turtles I didn't really see.

It was only a few minutes of a video clip—baby turtles hatching in the dunes and scurrying down the beach toward the sea. Of course they don't know why they are in such a rush, but as the camera pulls out, we can see they are hurrying because the circling seagulls are hungry.

The slower ones unwillingly give themselves to sustain the birds. I imagine the baby turtles know nothing of seagulls or survival, they only feel the air on their backs, the sand on their belly as they head downhill.

How do they know where the sea is? Is it the smell of the moisture? The sound of the waves? The gravity of the moon? Regardless, without thinking, their whole bodies know the sea is their only possible life. There is no hesitation.

Most of the little ones we see make it to the waves and unerringly dive in. Immediately at home, they swim confidently, for the first time ever, out toward the depths. No need for swimming lessons or orienteering instructions. They swim without thought or separation. Swimming is their manifestation of turtle wisdom—truly miraculous from the outside and, I suspect, totally unknown to the tiny actors.

For thousands of miles and many years, they will blindly and perfectly reenact the pattern of knowing called *turtle*.

I am beginning to suspect that we are all guided as perfectly as the baby turtles. As we make our plans and live our lives, there is a wisdom that sustains and guides us—the vast intelligence that we can live directly but only know implicitly.

There is a Native American poem that sings of this possibility that we so rarely see: Why do I go about pitying myself when all the time I am being carried on great winds across the sky?

Seeing the sweet and certain baby turtles, I imagine the possibility of trusting these great winds of my life more fully.

Travel Snacks and Love

I VISITED MY SISTER in Pennsylvania last week. As I was leaving for the four-hour drive home, she presented me with a bag of travel snacks. It was a cornucopia of treats—tasty cookies with chocolate on top, sweet and crunchy Kind bars, pretzels, an apple, an orange, chocolate chips, raisins, and a bottle of water. Everything a traveler could want. And it was accompanied by a detailed note of description and love.

Pulling out of her driveway I felt safe and protected—as if I were a first-grader again and my mother had just packed me a lunch laced with her magic love-power to protect me through the battles of the day.

Though today it was in a plastic bag rather than in the metal rocket ship lunch box I had in first grade, I was ready once again to go off to slay dragons and rescue fair damsels.

When I thanked my sister, she said it was a pleasure for her to think about and prepare this sustenance for me. I was touched by the love of her actions and words.

How unexpected.

Not the fact of her love, but the possibility of allowing it to penetrate the armor of my usual busyness.

Such a treasure available to me—just for the receiving.

Choosing Life

EARLIER THIS WEEK, I was leafing through a magazine at a Catholic retreat center where I was leading a workshop for a group of Episcopal priests.

For some reason, the citation from Deuteronomy 30:19 caught my attention: "I have set before you life and death... Choose life."

I've been reflecting on what it might mean—not in an abstract way, but what does it have to do with my experience of my life? What does it mean to *choose life*, not in a dramatic way that might happen in the movies, but right here where I am—right now, writing these words—or going out into the cold morning to refill the birdfeeder?

Many years ago I had an extraordinary experience in which I felt that we do indeed have the capacity to choose to live or choose to die—not just at the level of choosing to kill ourselves through an act of violence, but in a moment-to-moment way. At the deepest level, we are all choosing life at every moment.

Death only happens when the organism that we call ourselves stops making this choice.

Now whether this is "true" or not is not as interesting to me as the possibility that we have already chosen life. Each one of us who continues to breathe in and breathe out has made this astonishing choice. The choice has not been made by the "me" who thinks and plans but rather by the "me" who keeps the heart beating even when I am asleep—the me who decided to fall in love with and marry Melissa rather than any one of the other human beings in the world.

So then the questions get quite juicy: Who is this "me" that has already chosen life while "I" keep complaining about the circumstances in which I find myself?

And how do I align the "me" who thinks and plans with this deeper one who is already, constantly, and indiscriminately choosing life?

The Morning After

THIS COLD MORNING I WAKE SLOWLY—like an accident victim regaining consciousness. I wander through the *bardo* of coming into being.

Lying still with my head on the soft pillow, I consider incarnating one more time.

Where am I now? Who am I this time?

Without looking, I scan my body for clues—for some beginning point. Chest, belly, heart, throat, head, legs, arms. How is it *this* time? What's the diagnosis? What's the prognosis?

As both doctor and patient—I carefully take in all the information before jumping to judgment. "It's not so bad," I finally tell myself. "The heaviness in your chest is just a slight case of your-team-lost-the-Super-Bowl-in-the-final-moments-because-the-other-team-made-an-exceptionally-brilliant-play. You should make a full recovery by late morning."

I sigh, squirm, and wiggle under the warm covers

before rolling over, swinging my feet to the hard wood floor, and weaving my way into the bathroom to pee.

Enough Is Not Enough

Even longtime New Englanders are beginning to complain about the white fluffy stuff falling out of the sky.

A headline in the *Boston Globe* reports "city officials" as saying "Enough Is Enough." Apparently, though, this is not true. Enough is not enough.

Here at the temple, our parking lot is growing smaller with each successive snowfall—the snow banks higher and thicker.

Soon we'll have a walled parking lot—maybe it will become a secret garden—we'll keep it a private place that only certain people can find their way into. And perhaps inside the season will change— the falling snow will become a soft mist that the morning sun will burn off. And we'll all take our jackets off—though we won't let anyone know. We'll take off our jackets and maybe even our shirts—to dance slowly in the warm sun. We'll dance with the sweet currents of energy. Sometimes we'll even fly—become birds and fly though the sky with a wild freedom.

Ahhhhh—that's better.

But this morning, there is the freedom and grace of snow shoveling and snow blowing to be done. Bundle up, start the engine, make a lot of noise, and do some real work.

As I head out, I recall a friend talking about his father who is now confined to bed and near death. His father said he was sad to not be out shoveling.

So, thankful for this body that still has the energy to work and play outside, I'll get my morning exercise moving the white stuff around.

Remembering

LAST NIGHT, a friend told me of a poem that says that the meaning of our lives is in the ordinary things.

It reminded me of someone I heard interviewed about the grieving process who said that what we miss most when a loved one dies are the everyday things—not the wild romance and the moments of passion, but the livingness of each day.

And another friend who is in a relationship with an uncertain future is appreciating that the circumstance of really not being able to plan a future has brought both her and her partner into the moment more deeply.

So this morning, I am grateful for the fat handle of my diner-white mug, warm and filled with hot tea, as I climb the golden wood of the back stairs. An old poster of a brown Buddha greets me at the landing and through the window I see the streetlights across the road—still on though the dawn has already come.

Just this one step.

Foot rises—miraculously really—and my slippered foot slides onto the next shiny wooden plank.

One ancient Zen master says that no matter how far a bird flies, it never finds the end of the sky.

This morning I see again that this luminous awareness of the ordinary goes on forever—vast, effortless, and without limit. Hiding in plain sight, this gift of life is given fully in each moment—in each day.

Ah yes, now I remember.

Reluctant Adventurer

WE'RE PLANNING our first residential *ango* retreat here at the temple. Traditionally, an ango is a three-month period of intensive meditation practice and training. It's a Buddhist practice that goes back to the days when the Buddha gathered with his disciples during the rainy season to study and practice while the roads were impassable. But since I'm the chief organizer and leader, and I still have a day job as a life coach, I decided that three weeks would be plenty long.

Last fall, when we put it on the calendar, it seemed like a grand idea—slightly romantic and a great opportunity for extended meditation.

But as we get closer I'm beginning to feel a little less sure. Twenty-one days of silence and sitting still? Yikes! I'm committed to meditation, but this seems rather daunting. Will my body be able to do this? Will I be able to find my way? What if I can't do it?

This sense of queasy apprehension is familiar to

me. It seems to be part of how I move forward in my life.

I have a lively imagination and some innate confidence that I will find a way to make things happen. So I commit to things that call to me—to lead this retreat, to speak to a large group of people, to go to a distant place to teach a workshop—without knowing exactly how I will do it. But I've noticed that my self-assurance diminishes in direct proportion to the nearness of the event itself.

The planning is exciting—to imagine what might be possible fills me with energy. However, as the event gets closer, I begin to wonder why I was so arrogant to think I could accomplish this new task. Packing to set off on a new adventure, I'm almost always wishing I could just stay home and play in the garden.

Beginning a workshop or retreat for a new group, I often question my competence and wonder how I will ever get through.

But though there are difficulties and discomforts, I am consistently rewarded by my travels and adventures.

Stepping across the threshold of discomfort, I find new territories and experiences that enrich and deepen my life. I have come to consider myself a reluctant adventurer.

So I take this queasy feeling in the pit of my stomach not as a sign that I'm headed in the wrong direction or that the ango is a bad idea, but rather that I am stepping into the next adventure.

I'm reminded of the lovely Picasso quote: "I am always doing that which I do not know how to do in order to learn how to do it."

Feeling Rather Brilliant

WINTER STILL CLINGS to the bare branches but the light is coming back.

The light is coming back!

I can feel it in my body. It's not just that the days are longer—it's that the sun is stronger. I don't know this by looking to see how high the sun is over the horizon at noon—I know it in my very cells.

This intelligence of my body—so vast and subtle, a web of pure functioning—doesn't question its competence. The heart pumps, the blood cells receive the oxygen in the lungs and offer it freely wherever needed.

Never still, always in motion—this body, always dying and recreating itself.

The food I eat becomes me. I know how to transform broccoli and Brussels sprouts into a human body—I just put them in my mouth, move my jaw up and down while using the soft fleshy friend of the tongue to carefully position the green bits so that the white enamel-coated bony protuberances, lined up so meaningfully—both sides top and bottom—crush them, careful not to catch the tongue on the down-bite, then...

...well it's a long story and, in truth, though I do it every day, I don't really know how it happens.

But this pure functioning—the coordination of billions of processes, simultaneously—all happens effortlessly while my amazing prefrontal cortex, whose electrical impulses I generally consider to be "me," is thinking deep thoughts about whether steel-cut oats or cold cereal would taste better for breakfast.

Grumbling

THROAT SORE, BODY TIRED. I wake up late still grumbling about the darkness of daylight savings time. I'm grumbling about most everything this morning.

I don't like this tiredness.

What's that weird feeling in my ear?

The theme of the last two days—in individual meetings in Zen, in coaching, and now in my life—has been being with what we don't want to be with. This reminds me of the Buddha's first teaching of the fact of suffering and the second teaching that this suffering comes from our opinion about how things should be.

Again and again, I find myself encountering something that I am quite certain should not be the way it is—a tiredness, a difficulty, a discomfort. This certainty arises so quickly that I hardly notice it as opinion and I continue on my not-so-merry way in the unconscious certainty that "This couldn't be my one true life." It doesn't even occur to voice this out loud, because it seems so manifestly and obviously true.

So I try to fix it, move away from it, or just space out.

But as I begin to notice this experience of wanting it to be different, to become aware of my opinion that it "should" be different, something shifts—a space arises—an interruption of the inertia of delusion.

And in this space, right where I am, I find something new and unnamable.

This morning, my great vow is to be with what is arising—the sore throat and the tiredness as well as my opinion that it should be otherwise. Even the grumbling is redeemed when I remember to look here.

A Sense of Things to Come

IN THE EARLY morning dark I sneak outside for a few minutes after I make my tea. It's been a night above freezing for the first time in months and the damp coolness in the air feels alive to me.

Standing out on the porch swinging my arms in random directions, my body remembers spring—the dirt and possibility lying silently beneath the season's accretion of snow.

Yesterday, it was nearly sixty degrees and I spent part of my day digging in the snow bank that the plow has pushed up against the temple. My intention was to create a channel away from the foundation for the melting snow water to follow. It wasn't strictly necessary—a good idea—but no water in the basement yet. Preventative. Prophylactic.

But mostly for me.

To be outside—to be pushing the world around. A shovel full of snow thrown out over the parking lot to melt. A careful channel of water through the ice and snow.

When I was young and it rained really hard in the summer, the water would come down the gutters of our suburban street in torrents. My mother let us—I suspect even encouraged us—to play outside. Or was it that we were out playing and got drenched before we could get home and asked if we could stay outside? Either way we ended up totally wet.

Then, fearless of the rain, we walked up the street—delighting in our freedom of wetness.

I do want to be included in this world—to escape this persistent dream of separation. I want to wait for spring sprouting with the dignified patience of the bare trees.

But mostly these days I feel like an impatient sapling—dancing quickly in the breezes like a squirmy child: "Are we there yet? Is winter over? How much longer?"

Being Myself

IDENTITY IS the act of ongoing re-creation. Amid the cacophony of living and dying, each cell in my body is charged with the task of maintaining and replicating itself. Outside my window, the ovoid leaves of the rhododendron hold their shape—their cell walls separate inside from outside—clearly defining what is *leaf* and what is *world*. The buds, still tightly closed to the winter cold, will soon open up and flowers will emerge—not tulips, not daffodils, but rhododendron flowers—ruffled and almost overdone in their frilly pinkness.

And new leaves will be formed.

The rhododendron is rhododendroning—this is all it knows how to do.

I am like this too—I am David and I am Daviding.

Without thinking, my cells and my internal organs, my fingers and my brain, all know what to do.

All this living and dying and *selfing* going on while

I gather my water bottle and my bag with Zen-teacher gear to drive to Boston to lead a morning meditation.

Ango Breakdown

—————

IT'S DAY FOUR of our twenty-one-day meditation retreat, our *ango*.

Instead of sitting serenely in the meditation hall, I'm lying in my bedroom on the second floor of the temple feeling sick and sorry for myself.

I've got the flu, or bronchitis, but the real problem is not my body—it's this mind that keeps running around in painful circles. Everywhere I look, I see confirmation of my inadequacy.

I haven't planned this properly!

We'll probably have to cancel the rest of the retreat, and it's all my fault!

I know I'm caught in a painful realm, yet I can't seem to get free.

I try all of my spiritual tricks—paying attention to the breath, scanning the body, practicing loving-kindness, praying, calling out to the bodhisattva of compassion—nothing seems to make a difference. I have not been in a place this dark for many years.

My negative thinking and self-criticism feeds on itself and I feel powerless to stop it. All I can do is lie here and suffer.

By the midafternoon, I am so desperate that I call my wife, Melissa, and my Zen teacher, George. Neither are available so I leave tearful messages of struggle and despair on both their phones.

George is the first to call me back.

I am happy to hear his voice. He listens for a little and then says in a cheerful voice, "Wow, you're really in a dark place!" Though I had hoped he would be soothing and empathetic, his matter-of-factness and lightness reminds me that dark places like this are part of the landscape of intensive practice.

Doing deep spiritual work of almost any kind, we can count on meeting our demons. While it may sound romantic or noble when we read about the dark night of the soul, we all really know it is a fearsome place. In the moment, I still feel trapped and dark, and slightly resentful George isn't taking my pain more seriously—but I am also relieved.

Maybe I am not a failure—just a traveler in a dark place.

As Melissa said earlier that morning, "Honey, you're just sick."

George also suggests the possibility that I ask other people for help.

For some reason, this hadn't occurred to me.

That evening, still barely able to get out of bed, I ask three senior students to take over some of the major responsibilities of running the retreat. To my surprise and great relief, they all quickly and whole-heartedly say yes.

I feel both humbled and held.

I learn yet again that even though I am one of the leaders, I don't have to keep things going by myself. Others are willing and eager to help. Asking others to step in is not an exercise in delegation but an acknowledgment of my human limitations.

And most surprisingly is the realization that my breakdown, my failure, is part of what allows other people to step forward and give their gifts to the community.

My incapacity to always be the wise and fearless leader appears to be part of the gift I have to give this community.

SPRING

Clunking Heads with Buddha

TODAY IS THE DAY of my Dharma Transmission ceremony.

It's standing room only in the temple meditation hall on this unseasonably warm evening. Outside, winter's blanket of snow has only recently given way to brown earth and the first delicate white blossoms of early spring. The ceremony has begun and I'm up front, sitting between two of my favorite people in the whole world: my teacher George ("Zen Master Bomun") and my wife Melissa ("Zen Master Myozen"). I look around and see my aging parents, my now grown-up daughter, and the delighted faces of friends, students, and colleagues.

Surprisingly, these people seem to hold some unreasonable affection for me. Their palpable positive regard gently but unambiguously undermines my most ancient delusions of isolation and inadequacy. In this ritualized moment of community, I know for certain that I am not alone and have never been alone. All I can do is smile. And my smile is returned over and over and over.

George gives me the robe and bowl that were given to him by his teacher. These are the traditional symbols of a Dharma Transmission in Zen. We kneel and bow to each other—accidentally clunking heads as we stand even though we have carefully rehearsed this moment. This is the transmission—the clunking of heads from the Buddha, through the Indian teachers and Chinese teachers and Korean teachers—now given to me by my American teacher.

I thank George, thank my parents, thank Melissa, thank my daughter, and thank everyone assembled.

Such an honor and such a responsibility. How not to get lost in the title and in the projections? How to use this official role to continue to lead others toward their own hearts? How to keep walking ahead in my own journey without getting stuck in imagining I have reached the end?

But in this moment, I am fully satisfied.

The true transmission is happening here, among all of us.

It is clearly not just about me.

Each one of us exists only through this continuous giving and receiving—this heart-to-heart transmission from our parents, our friends, our teachers—from our whole life. This essence of life, this peace that passes understanding, this love—this is what naturally arises between human being. Mostly, we're too busy or scared or lost to notice. But tonight, the air is thick with appreciation. Something unmistakable is happening. Right here.

After the ceremony I eat delicious cake and hug as many people as I can.

I smile and smile.

By the end of the evening, my cheeks are sore.

Later on, I go upstairs, take off my fancy robes, put on my pajamas, and go to bed.

Speaking Softly

PRETTY MUCH every morning these days, I walk slowly round the temple grounds with my head down. A friend interrupted this ritual perambulation the other day and apologized for disturbing my meditation.

But I'm not really meditating, I'm just keeping track of what's new here in this particular place.

Almost every day some new green-tipped sprout asserts its still liveliness through the surface of the hard earth. Each one astonishes me and I almost involuntarily greet my new companion with a few words of welcome. I suppose it's silly of me, talking to these mute green beings, but I can't help myself.

I do, however, in the interest of propriety, keep my voice low and my comments brief: "Oh, there you are. Good to see you."

Though these silent green shoots are delicate, they manifest the mysterious and fierce power that animates the universe.

Through the winter cold these plants have rested in darkness without resisting. Now, in the warmth and light of these longer days, they appear as if from nowhere. None of the wisdom lost for the dying back, they emerge into the light once again new and remember perfectly the pattern of their growth.

And with each new sprout, I see the full flowering already here.

The pointed thrusting sprouts of the hosta contain the full spreading cascade of summer leaves.

The grass-like few green leaves of the Japanese iris are already elegant purple bird-like blossoms swaying on round stems.

And the tightly wound fiddlehead ferns, still close to the ground, proclaim the ancient unfurled fronds of lacy green to come.

It makes me happy to witness all this. I am conscious of my privilege to once again walk the spring earth and feel my kinship with these fine green fellows. We breath the same air and drink the same water.

And I know for sure, though it is most often just a whisper, that they too are speaking to me.

Cherry Blossoms at the Temple

LAST FALL, AS we were cutting back the overgrown garden near the front door of the temple, we found a weeping cherry tree.

It was hiding—choked by thorny vines and shaded by sumacs—but still alive.

We cut back the bramble and eventually designed the access ramp to wrap around this forgotten beauty.

As we worked through the fall, I kept imagining what these cascading green branches might look like covered with delicate pink spring blossoms. It wasn't a clear picture—it never is for me. The image was more like a feeling—a subtle and complex constellation of possibility. I imagined the tree as a fountain— the sturdy trunk as the uprising water and the blossoms as the white frothy water arcing gracefully out in every direction—falling freely to the ground.

Earlier in the week, I saw the first buds.

Yesterday, this tree of possibility came into full

bloom—both more spectacular and more ordinary than my imaginings.

Walking the ramp to view the tree from every side, I was filled with a bubbly energy of amazement. The excitement of fruition—that this vision had come to life, that this tree which had stood so silent through the winter could blossom forth with such delicate beauty. And yet the cars on the nearby street kept speeding past, and after taking a few pictures, I simply went back to the rest of my busy day.

I must remember to spend some time today sitting with the tree.

These moments of blossoming are precious partly because they are so fleeting. The Japanese have tradition called this *hanami*—flower viewing. Families, workers from factories, all kinds of people will come with their blankets, picnic lunches, and bottles of sake to sit under the cherry trees. They talk and sing songs as the children run around and normal life goes on.

And the delicate spring blossoms broadcast their lovely and ephemeral teaching.

Instructions to Self for Wandering

WANDER RELIGIOUSLY with no apparent destination.

Allow animals to lick your nose.

Sail on the puddles in the sidewalk.

Keep just enough of your wits about you to make mental notes as you fall slowly to the ground.

Notice that the journey down is a thing of exacting beauty—weightless forever.

In the falling, find a whole new world.

Choose the in-between and disappear fully into the middle way.

Now, with nothing to defend, you are free to love everything you meet.

Coming Home

THE CREAMY GOLDEN daffodils are vividly alive this morning as I wander down the brick path behind the temple. I see for myself how the soft sun shines through their translucent petals. Later today the petals will be opaque again. But in their momentary morning glow, I fall in love again with this blue-green fleshy living mother planet we call earth.

I feel like a single-celled bacterium that has taken up permanent residence in the welcoming darkness of my intestinal track—content to do my part in the ongoing work of digestion even though I know nothing of "food" or "nourishment" or the impossibly larger multicelled biped that believes itself to be "David."

Sustained and sustaining the larger fabric, each of us is a particle containing the whole.

We each come forth unknowingly and are effortlessly sustained by an unimaginable grace.

Not just the sweet grace of morning daffodils but

the shiny, dangerous grace of the poison ivy beginning to climb the garage wall. The rising and falling grace of all that comes into being, manifests in the particular, and then passes away. This is the effortless functioning of the Dharma that includes all my stories of success and failure, as well as the damp bricks under my feet as I walk the garden path.

This afternoon my true love is coming home and I am grateful for the chance to see her once more.

Hosta Love

A FRIEND OF MINE recently informed me that high-class gardeners regard hosta with some disdain. I'm not sure why this is so, but it has redoubled my appreciation of the hosta I brought with me to the temple grounds. None of them are in full leaf yet, but at least a dozen plants have sent up their determined shoots.

Last fall, I transplanted as many different hosta plants and varieties as I could reasonably take from my old garden while preserving it for the new owners (who I hope are appreciative of all I left behind).

There's the two-toned gold and green hosta I originally got from the house across town that was my office for thirteen years. One of the former owners had visited us when he was quite an elderly man. He was happy to reminisce about the gardens he loved. When I enthused over the variegated hosta still growing vigorously beside the house, he proudly told me they came from his mother's house.

Then there's the huge dusky green–leafed hosta I bought from a roadside vegetable stand. Several large bare-rooted plants were there wilting in the afternoon August sun—clearly just dug up from someone's garden and not looking very promising. I bought one of these lifeless plants with low expectations. To my surprise, the next year, the plant grew to three feet high and nearly five feet across. Each leaf was larger than it had any reasonable right to be—as if it were purposely taking the whole leaf idea to another level—like the potter I knew who decided to make four-foot-high teapots. Delight of unexpected proportions!

But my favorite hosta is the one with crinkled variegated leaves of white and green. I can't remember where it came from, but it lived by the side door in the white rock garden. Each year it threw out a profusion of large and textured leaves. Quietly extravagant and elegant, it sat before the clay Buddha under the dogwood who greeted us every day as we left the house. I divided the plant several times to have more of it elsewhere and it would always fill in as if it hadn't even noticed.

And here, this spring, I am enjoying once again the slow motion dance of the sprouting, the rising, and the promised unfurling of these various and delicate-leaved hosta. I feel like a child who endlessly delights in the same storybook. Parents' boredom with the repetition is no match for his familiar excitement with the turning of each page. Habitual pictures and expected words delight some deep part of my brain. Though I know what's coming—because I know what's coming—I allow myself to be carried away each time. With the ritual of each repetition, everything is set right. With each spring, I am reborn, and the growingness of life itself inches more deeply into the center of my heart.

I admit there's a little extra excitement this year because I can't quite remember which hosta I put where.

But with my short-term memory vanishing at an increasingly steady pace, I have a lot of this kind of entertainment these days.

Where did I put the keys that I just had in my hands five minutes ago? There's the slight rising panic and the occasional lovely pleasure of finding them in some obvious place. Oh, I put the keys in my shoes so I wouldn't put them down on some random surface in the house. In the finding, a moment of relief. I thank my former self for having the wisdom and foresight to put them down someplace I might look.

Anyway, I love my low-class hosta. I am waiting and watching with great pleasure. I'm eager to see what comes next, and I want this slow, cool spring to last forever.

Meanwhile, the new leaves on the crab apple tree outside my window are like tiny green flags waving underneath the quiet fireworks of white blossoms.

Manifesting Wisdom

THIS GLORIOUS SPRING MORNING has taken me by surprise.

Wandering through my garden I'm delighted with my old friends that have come back to once again manifest the wisdom of their green amazement.

The lacy leaves of the bleeding heart rise nearly to my knee. The soon-to-be-elegant leafy hosta break ground as chubby spears lancing upward.

And forget-me-nots that have run wild in the garden like five-year-olds at recess are now recognizable low clumps that hold out their tiny white balls of flower buds.

Everything knows exactly what to do—knows how to give way to the next stage of itself—leaving behind the safety of dark winter stillness for the uncertain and necessary venture of spring becoming.

The Moment of Fullness

THE CRAB APPLE TREE that was covered with delicate white blossoms last week was bedraggled in yesterday's rain and wind.

The few petals previously dislodged by the bees have been joined by countless others now littering the ground.

The peak of blooming that I had been carefully waiting for has already come and gone.

That exact moment of fullness is now well past, and I can't tell you when it happened.

The excitement of the first flower buds led to amazing openings and the sweet delicacy of a thousand flowers filling the sky just outside my window. For almost two weeks I watched the silent drama. And I kept wondering—is *this* the moment? The moment where it can't get any better? Where there is no more room for ascension and one direction turns into another?

Even in the watching I suspected the impossibility

of finding what I was looking for. Like a mountain summit on a foggy day—we find the peak only when the descent begins. But unlike a mountain, there is no retracing the steps to yesterday's blossoming fullness.

Still some petals linger, insisting on more time.

But most have accomplished their falling—giving way to the fruitful gestation of summer and tiny red "apples" of the fall.

This growing work of the coming warmer season, I have to take on faith and memory. This new business of fruition is even slower, even more quiet than the blossoming itself—and is quickly forgotten amid the profusion of leaves and the busyness of life.

Breaking Apart

IN ONE OF HIS dense and rewarding books, anthropologist and Zen student Gregory Bateson writes that the term *cliché* was derived from a French printers' term for a mechanical device that "clinched" individual letters together in repeated phrases. These "clichés" were used to save time in typesetting. Rather than assemble the individual letters each time the phrase was used, printers just grab a clinched bunch, a *cliché*.

Bateson points out that to use the letters of a cliché to create new words and new meanings first requires that the cliché be broken apart. He suggests that our learning is like this—that our understandings of our selves and our world are bits of information we hold together in a fixed way. Learning often requires that our old perspectives be broken apart before we can be open to what is new and unfolding.

The chaos and upset of our lives is often part of this breaking apart of what we thought we knew. It most often feels wrong or bad, but this disorganization creates the space for what is creative and alive to be known. As we can tolerate the place of loosening the grip of our certainty, this problematic place becomes the source of the solution—and we are released into the new world of this actual moment.

Of course, in a heartbeat, our new understanding becomes the next cliché—fine to use as long as it serves, but needing to be broken apart again in service of our next learning.

The Zen tradition has a time-worn phrase for this: Today's enlightenment becomes tomorrow's delusion.

Familiar Suspicion

It's a little cool to be out on the back porch so early in the morning, but I can't resist the green suffusion of this spring morning.

A blanket over my legs, I sit with my comforting cup of tea in the bouncy deck chair that used to belong to my grandmother. Birds squabble near the hanging feeder while the nearby prehistoric ferns seem to still long for the dinosaurs' return.

And I wonder at the generosity of life.

The generosity of sight and smell—of imagination and locomotion. My fingers moving across the keyboard demonstrate a percussive intelligence that far outweighs these simple thoughts that leave their traces in these words on the screen. I recognize the flexible pinkish tubes as "mine," yet I have no idea how each one knows the position and timing of its duty. Nor do I have any idea where and how the thoughts arise in me and how I choose one over another.

I would say that I am writing, yet the "I" who is writing and how he does it is fully hidden from me.

I come back to my familiar suspicion that this one who I imagine myself to be is only the merest of coverings—a thin veneer self masquerading as prime mover.

I must again confess the embarrassing truth that I appear to myself as God: from this deck chair, unless I pay very close attention, I am quite sure it is all up to me. My job is to make sure everything goes right—to think and feel the right things, to make good choices that lead to good results, and to ensure the smooth function of the universe.

But this morning I catch a glimpse of the imposter and am relieved to step out of this weighty and impossible job.

With no plan the squirrels delight in the free seed scattered beneath the bird feeder. And in this moment, I appreciate that the plan of each finger and the arising of each thought comes for free from the mysterious source that gives life to all.

Quick Realization

THE UNIVERSE GIVES US every opportunity to realize that the personal identity we hold so fiercely, the things we possess, and the plans we have are all provisional. Sometimes it happens slowly—like the slow smoothing of rough stones as they tumble against other stones in a streambed.

Sometimes it happens in an instant, like it did for me earlier this week on the Mass Pike.

I was in bumper-to-bumper, stop-and-go traffic, headed for the airport last Tuesday morning. The car ahead slowed suddenly and I braked hard. Just as I was feeling relieved that I had been able to stop in time, I was shocked by a huge impact from behind and realized the car behind me had just plowed into my trunk. And just as that realization came, I felt another impact in front, which was me being pushed into the back bumper of the car in front of me.

Both the car and I were intact enough to drive home—though I have spent part of this week making visits to healers of various sorts and the car was scored a "total loss" by my insurance company. Now that the vividness is fading, one of my lasting impressions is the drive home.

I was trying to process the shock of the accident. My world and my plans had been changed irrevocably. I felt personally attacked by the universe—scared of the physical damage to the car and uncertain about my physical condition. I kept replaying the sequence of events—wondering about my part in them and played several varieties of the "If only…" game.

But what I remember most is seeing the blue sky above the green trees and feeling grateful to be alive—grateful for the air coming in and out of my lungs.

Just driving down the endless road looking out over the crinkled hood of my car was, for that brief moment, perfectly enough.

Spiraling Toward God

YESTERDAY I MADE my daily pilgrimage to my morning glory seedlings in the planters under the bare pergola on the access ramp. A week and a half ago, I carefully ran ten lines of brown twine from a horizontal wire near the planters to the top of the pergola. My plan was that each of the ten morning glory plants would climb up one of the strings.

The seedlings have been getting nearly big enough to train onto these strings.

I lean over the taller ones toward the appropriate string—like bringing a newborn to her mother's breast. You can't really "teach" a baby to suck on the breast but you can awaken his inborn knowing. The infants without this sucking knowledge inscribed in their DNA did not survive to pass on their genes. So I have been bringing the sprouting runners over to touch the string—hoping they will get the idea—like how gentle rubbing of the baby's cheek makes her turn her head and "look for" the breast.

Most days, when I have gone back to check, the plants have righted themselves—spurning the string support for the free-form vertical. But yesterday, two of them finally got the idea. They had each made one spiral trip around the string and were headed for the top. I was unreasonably proud and delighted to see the results of my careful planning and coaxing. And I was amazed by the intelligence of these plants.

How was this rising wisdom contained in the small round seed I planted in damp soil a month ago? I suppose the leaves themselves are miracle enough—but this capacity to sense the string and to begin the climb—a dumb intelligence beyond understanding.

I went out again this morning to look.

Now there are three beginning the climb and two have made several trips around—and are now spiraling upward. And I pray that our lives too may be spiraling upward in ways beyond our knowing. Is there a string that is set for each of us that runs toward God—toward the source of our lives?

I suspect that the aliveness of our lives is the string.

We can't really "know" what the string is—just like I don't think the morning glory has any conception of "string" or "pergola" or "David is such a clever gardener." But the growing tip of the plant knows enough to curl around whatever it meets.

I pray that I have the same cellular intelligence and can respond appropriately when the universe gently rubs my cheek so that I can turn toward what nourishes me.

The Birthday Gift

THOUGH I GENERALLY consider myself to be emotionally sensitive, I'm actually not that into sharing my feelings. It almost always feels like complaining and even I find it boring. I grew up believing that people weren't really interested in what was going on inside me. As long as I behaved reasonably well, everyone seemed happy.

The deep feelings of loneliness and confusion I lived with were just what everyone felt. Since there was no solution, these things were best kept to oneself.

But the other day was my sister Ellen's birthday and she called me as she was in the car on a trip to see our father. I wished her happy birthday and got a quick update on her sick puppy, who is now on the mend. Then she said, "I just want to hear you talk for a little. Tell me about how things are for you." A stunning invitation—especially coming from someone who is coping with a protracted and ongoing recovery from serious head trauma and whose husband (my brother-in-law) has permanently left the workforce due to the increasing effects of multiple sclerosis.

And she asks *me* to talk about what's really going on in my life.

From one perspective, how can I open my mouth? Compared to what she has been through over the past five years, I have no right to complain about anything. And yet, in spite of the many blessings of my life, I still struggle.

Even the things I love regularly turn into huge burdens. The beautiful temple becomes the sinkhole that takes all my time and money and where things are never done. My coaching practice becomes too busy or I get scared something will happen and it will fall apart. The many people coming in and out of the temple shift from being friends and colleagues to being critics and problems to be solved. And my book project changes from being a fascinating and revealing exploration to a hopeless cause.

But she asked, and I knew she really wanted to know about me. I tell her of my fears and insecurities around "writing a book"—that I won't be able to do it. That I don't know how to do it. That I won't get it right. That the book will be too much of my ego and professional posing and won't be the message from my heart that I long to share.

Ellen listens and is clearly glad to have me talk

about my troubles. She doesn't compare or minimize but meets me in my place of confusion and sadness. Talking with her, I feel permission to be lost and in that permission begin to feel less wrong. Speaking of my ongoing "failure" shifts it ever so slightly from the clear reality to simply one way to look at what is going on. She reminds me that the book is already here, already has become a gift to help me clarify my life.

"Everything has its own time," she says.

We can't make things grow faster than they grow. When it's time for something to come into being, there is no way you could stop it.

Of course I already know this—I just keep forgetting it applies to me.

Ellen so clearly loves me and accepts my struggle—not as the truth of the situation, but the truth of my feeling. She believes not a trace of my story of personal inadequacy.

I am comforted and heartened.

Just before we hang up Ellen says, "Thank you. This is the best birthday present I could have gotten."

And I remember once again that my value to the world is not about being wise, or compassionate, or working really really hard.

In my sister's heartfelt thanks, I'm reminded that my full humanness is the gift I bring. Remarkably, this includes the parts of myself and my life I find most difficult.

In speaking the truth of what I struggle with, I relinquish my often fierce grasp on playing the part of the wise older brother. My little sister gets to be the one who is loving and understanding—who comforts me in my fears and insecurities.

We are mutually released.

In this simple phone call we both become the giver, the receiver—and the birthday gift.

I Feel Like a Tomato Seedling

I FEEL LIKE A TOMATO SEEDLING emerging from the earth after many days in the damp darkness of the ground of myself.

Those uncounted days are an eternity for the tomato seed.

The unfamiliar tickling of moisture calls to something inside me—the deep ache of longing for something unimaginable. All I know of me is flat and round—a small disc of unremarkable color.

Everything else is a scarlet dream—a picture once glimpsed—a whispered fragment of a story.

Then the terror and wonder starts. The wet coolness of the earth begins to dissolve me. Here are urges I have never felt. I try to resist but am powerless. I can't hold myself together. Saying my last prayers, I allow myself to be split open. Breaking apart, I discover anew that I am not what I thought. I feel myself going up and down at the same time.

The vertical urge toward a power above appears as a single stem whose full function is, as of yet, hidden from me. And in the other direction is a gentler, finer urge downward. Little white threads spreading quietly deeper into the soil to receive necessary nourishment from this unknowing darkness.

And now—breaking ground—a tender stalk with a few small leaves.

Expecting immediate tomatoes, I am disappointed with my meager green showing. Yet even here, the juicy crimson globes of the future may be hiding— invisible—biding their time, waiting to manifest.

Letting the seedling be the seedling, myself be myself, is the work of the moment. To abandon the seedling for not being the tomato is to mistake the timing of things.

The roots are these days of writing and reflecting. Giving myself permission again and again to wander without knowing the destination. This seems to be the only path with aliveness. My notebooks bulge with pages of wonderings and noticings—with the shufflings and shapings of now familiar ideas and frameworks.

They look nothing like a book.

But there is some form that I sense emerging— some sprouts that are poking their tender heads through the earth—promising some as yet unformed and delicious fruit. I pray for the faith and determination to keep walking ahead—to keep doing that which I do not know how to do.

Morning Glory Update

THE MORNING GLORIES have climbed from the shallow rectangular boxes to the top of the pergola.

Reaching the summit, they keep on climbing.

Failing to find support other than each other, the tendrils fall in graceful arcs back to their original rising string and climb once again. The neat preliminary geometry of my ten strings has been wonderfully overgrown with the green energy of twisting and climbing.

It turns out that along with rising up toward the sun, the morning glories also know how to circumambulate.

There must be some biological message that happens on contact—the cells that are touched by the string begin to grow more slowly or the cells on the other side to grow more quickly. This seemingly small wisdom allows the morning glories to enlist whatever is at hand to support their upward mission of sun gathering.

I imagine the ten small round black seeds I started with are quite proud of themselves. With no legs or hands, no prefrontal cortex or apparent income stream, they have accomplished amazing things.

First was enlisting the commercial grower to tend, select, and package them.

Then they dreamed themselves into my head to convince me to buy the package (it was their alluring blue photo on the front that made me do it) then to tenderly put them in little wet homes of dirt to allow them to sprout.

Then was the building of the handicap access ramp and the pergola (which of course had to start long before).

And finally transplanting them to the flower boxes and the stringing of the twine supports—carefully secured near the sprouts and to the top of the pergola that allowed them to rise and turn.

I like the tangled mass of green with tendrils flaying out like unruly wisps of hair.

And I'm still waiting to see the deep blue morning glory blossoms that are planted in my mind.

The Numbers

EVERY MORNING when I write, I begin by putting the date in the upper left-hand corner—like an obedient schoolboy who has learned to start each assignment with the correct heading.

And often I'm amazed that the low numbers of the beginning of the month pass so quickly to the fat middle teens and then turn into the high twenties as the month end approaches. Like an old movie showing the passing of time—the daily pages of the calendar are blown away faster and faster.

These numbers at the top of my pages race through their progressions—the first number, the month, slowly marches the circle from one to twelve while the second daily number dashes to thirty or so, puts his hands on his hips like an exhausted sprinter, then goes back to the starting line to begin again at one.

And the years, I can hardly think of them.

Just as I get really used to '12, I know '13 will come to take me by surprise.

Once, long ago, I saw the end of a bigger cycle—from '99 to '00. How astonishing! But I know these big numbers will never come again for me.

A young friend called me yesterday to discuss the dimensions of trust and intimacy in relationships. She speaks of disappointment and difference, and wonders when compromise is good for the soul and when it is merely lack of courage. Having no answers, I wonder with her—exploring this familiar territory that is always new. With no resolutions, I reassure her that these questions are indeed the landscape of relationship itself.

Now in my fifty-ninth year, now with this practice of writing, now on this computer screen—I see the days going by.

Not true.

I *imagine* I see the days going by. I don't really.

It's just the numbers and the older man who occasionally catches my attention in the mirror.

But the boy is still here and endlessly eager to explore the backyard. So I continue to notice and write about the silly things like morning glories that thrill me with the magic tricks they have done for years and years.

An hour has nearly passed in writing and tinkering with even these words.

I know this by the numbers in the upper right-hand portion of my screen.

Writing, I feel my way on instinct—always trying to find the beating heart of things. It's a delicate procedure, and often the flashing firefly I catch at dusk turns out to just be a dark bug in the light of morning.

Logic, apparently, is not enough.

I am learning to trust my senses and allow the dancing of time to teach me what I need to know.

Instructions
for an Ordinary Symphony

GATHER TEN THOUSAND PEOPLE.

Give each person two leaves.

(Make sure you have a variety of leaf shapes and sizes—some round and some angular, some the size of quarters and some the size of a pro basketball player's hands.)

Spread these people out randomly in a quarter mile radius.

Have them wait for your signal.

Gather several hundred cars and drivers.

(Again, variation is most essential.)

Have them wait out of sight—half of them wait to the east of the house and half wait to the west.

And use other vehicles too—mostly cars, but large trucks too—and make sure some of the trucks are filled with something heavy (we need that deep rumbling bass as they accelerate from the red light).

Have them all wait for your signal.

Now give the signal. (It should be grand and unmistakable.)

Leaf people: hit your two leaves against each other. Vary the rhythm and timing of your leaf striking. It must come and go like the wind. Let yourself feel the timing.

Drivers: start your vehicles at specific intervals then drive by in front of the house. Mix in the occasional truck. Come singly and in clumps. (Pay attention to the traffic light nearby. The idling is important.) And truck drivers: don't forget that lovely loud downshift to decelerate. (We need variation to enhance the softer sound of smaller cars.)

And don't forget the birds.

Position some in the trees nearby with loud squawks and have some so far away you can barely hear them.

Now shake the leaves. Have the rustling start on one side of the space and then go to the other. Have that indescribably soft sound begin and end quickly— then have it go on longer and slowly diminish.

Now a car.

Now several birds.

Have them seem to be engaging in a conversation. Make it be of some importance.

More leaves hitting against each other.

Now the slamming of a car door and the starting of an engine.

Don't stop—keep this music going night and day, constantly vary the timing and the intensity.

WE'VE ALL BEEN WAITING SO LONG to hear this unrivaled masterpiece.

Bee in Morning Glories

IF I WERE A BEE, I would want to spend my time
upside-down, stuck in a morning glory—with my
head buried in the sweetness and my body held on
every side by the softest fabric.

I'd willingly give up all my buzzing and dart-
ing around for a few moments of this rapture of
sweetness.

I'd be careful not to spend too long there—I
wouldn't want the other bees to question my moral
character or my commitment to the community.

On second thought, I'd not be careful.

I'd risk it all to spend a morning held in the middle
of the blue loveliness. A single morning would be a
lifetime in heaven.

Other bees would fly by and be surprised.

They would probably think the less of me for my
wanton abandon.

But perhaps not—perhaps they would simply
be too busy to notice me, just a minor aberration,

barely remembered on their way to more important business.

In the end, I wouldn't get much nectar, just a drop or two—but it would be worth it.

Ending my reverie I would stagger back to the hive and give my meager contribution.

No awards and no stories of great achievement.

I would listen silently as others justly tell of their accomplishments.

The other bees would have no use for me—the quiet one of little contribution. This would be fine with me. I'd keep dreaming of greater things—softer things— things that come and go and are beyond measure.

The next day, I might do it totally differently. This time just one moment in each flower—a blissful moment—the moment of touching my tongue to the sweetness and me still buzzing my way down its tender throat. I feel it all.

Each time, fully complete.

My bee fur gathers the dusty yellow possibility of morning glories yet to come.

My face sticky with the sweetness of flower after flower.

Each blossom sings its own blue melody.

I listen to the calling.

I hear them clearly now—the siren songs of these azure blossoms nearly bursts my heart.

I am entranced and have no choice but to obey.

Blue blossom gives way to white throat—each blue funnel made just for me—made just for this morning, just for this moment of entry and touching.

A whole lifetime of giving and receiving.

Afterword

It's raining again.

Mostly I don't mind.

I love the sound of the drops all night long through my open window—greeting me softly as I cycle through the realms of sleep. Now I'm up and drinking my tea in the gray and windy morning.

It's a perfect day to have to do things inside.

Recently, I've been thinking about beauty and love. Not about the abstract concepts, but about the calling of something so deep in my heart that it can't be named. As much as I love doing things in the world, this place of depth and beauty is not about activity—or maybe it's rather that the activity of this place is a stillness that contains everything.

I'm noticing (again) that I can consciously turn toward this deep place out of love rather than duty.

Instead of working hard at one more thing, when I turn toward this depth it's like greeting a long-lost friend.

No need for words or doing.

It's a great and familiar pleasure just to be in each other's presence.

My wish for all of us is a greater appreciation of the grace of this beauty and love.

Maybe just a momentary noticing how we are sustained and drawn forward in our lives—beyond all our knowing plans.

Like adventurers lured on to explore the next mountain and then the next valley—this luminous world endlessly and effortlessly offers itself to us.

This truth never fails.

Acknowledgments

WRITING THIS BOOK has been mysterious, terrifying, and deeply rewarding. Most surprising to me as a relatively new writer is the realization that while writing is an individual act, it always occurs in a communal context. This book would not have come into being without the active support of so many friends, colleagues, students, and family members.

Marjorie Clay was my first writing coach who managed to teach me better grammar while making me feel articulate. My colleagues in the Dolphin Leadership group were unreasonably supportive when this book was just a wild dream. Two different groups of friends listened to early drafts and encouraged me to write about what I loved rather than what I thought I should write about. Focusing teacher and lifetime friend Julie Townsend helped me dream deeply and move forward at a critical junction. Hannah Alpert-Abrams believed this material could be a book and helped with the initial shaping. Ellen Novack offered a trained eye and heart to the nearly finished manuscript.

Trish Bartley, Florence Meleo-Meyer, and Mark Beckwith and Marilyn Olson all enthusiastically opened their lovely homes in beautiful places to allow me the space to write. Friend and colleague Tamara Scarlet-Lyon has been reading and appreciating my writing for many years now. She has also consistently challenged me to dive directly into the heartland. My life coach Anne Grete Mazziotta walked with me through this whole journey and has been delightfully sure of the outcome from the very beginning. James Ishmael Ford, my Zen collaborator, Dharma brother, and role model, has supported the life and practice from which this book springs. Josh Bartok, my editor at Wisdom Publications, was wise enough to say "Yes" to some very early chapters and reckless enough to say "Yes" again when this project took a new shape halfway through. Josh's support helped me to both clarify my larger intention and express it most directly in even the smallest details.

Then there are gifts that can never be repaid. My daughter Rachel—you are one of the great joys and inspirations of my life (not to mention invaluable technical support). My parents and siblings who appear in these reflections—your support and love have shaped and sustained my life. Without you, none of this would have been possible. My beloved Zen teacher George Bowman—your example and presence have opened the true treasury of the Dharma to me; I can only begin to express my gratitude to you in passing on to others what you have so generously given to me.

And to my beloved wife Melissa Myozen Blacker—fellow teacher, friend, lover, and everything. I cannot imagine this book, or this life, without you.

Companion Guide

Though this book is a collection of very personal observations and reflections, the point of it is not mainly about the author, but rather about the possibility of becoming more intimate with our own lives. This companion guide is intended as a tool to help you use some of the concepts and issues raised in the book as a way to come into deeper relationship with yourself and the world around you.

INTRODUCTION

One of the main themes of this book that David brings up in the **INTRODUCTION** is "the practice and study of this extraordinary experience we call ordinary life."

▸ **Reflect:** When have you experienced some "ordinary" part of your life in an extraordinary way?

▸ **Practice:** As you go through your day today, take the time to look around you. What if things are not just what you think they are? Notice what you have never noticed before.

▸ **Remember:** What we are longing for is hiding in plain sight.

The **INTRODUCTION** tells us, "At the heart of things, there is a truth that is always revealing itself. Whether we call it the Dharma, or God, or the universe, or aliveness— it is essentially ungraspable."

▸ **Reflect:** What word or what image do you use to refer to the part of your life that is beyond your understanding? And what role does this word or image play in your life?

▸ **Practice:** Right now, allow yourself to know that this truth is with you—in you and all around you. You can't earn it or deserve it, it simply is. Let this truth be here. Open your heart to this energy of possibility and aliveness. Allow yourself to receive what is already here.

▸ **Remember:** Everything reveals the mysterious truth of aliveness.

SUMMER

In "**FIRST DAY BACK**," David writes about his anxious morning mind, how challenging it is to work with, and how it finds problems wherever it looks.

▸ **Reflect:** What difficult mind-state do you fall into on a regular basis? What is it like when you are there? What are the bodily sensations, feelings, and thoughts that tend to accompany this place?

▸ **Practice:** Next time you are aware of being in a challenging mind-state, pause a moment and notice what you are feeling in your body. Allow yourself to be where you are. Don't try to fix anything or figure anything out. Sometimes just noticing what is actually here allows feelings and thoughts to shift and release in some way.

▸ **Remember:** You are not merely who you think you are. You are more than your anxious mind.

In "**FEAR AND FAITH**," David talks about the gap between what he knows—his faith in life's unfolding— and in what he experiences in his life.

▸ **Reflect:** What is a truth you know about life that you often forget? Be as specific as you can.

▶ **Practice:** Come up with a word, or a phrase, or an image that reminds you of this deep truth that you often forget. Write this down on a piece of paper and carry it in your pocket all day; perhaps post it on your refrigerator or computer screen. Look it at it many times during the day and repeat the words or call the image to mind. Breathe it in and go on with your day.

▶ **Remember:** The root of the word that is usually translated as "mindfulness" means "to recollect or remember." Be mindful of your own deep truth.

In "MEASURING THINGS," David relates the joy of a young boy playing with a tape measure that he doesn't really understand and "the impossibility of measuring this path of being human."

▶ **Reflect:** Where and when do you most often try to "measure" your progress as a human being? What if your opinions about yourself and your worth are essentially arbitrary and not trustworthy? What if you were free from having to measure up?

▶ **Practice:** For one day, give yourself a free pass. Go through your normal day, but intentionally do not judge yourself by any standard. Let things happen. Do what needs to be done, then go on to the next thing. Let yourself choose and respond without knowing why. Let yourself be happy or sad. Confused or clear. Busy or idle. At the end of the day, give yourself an A+ and consider what you have learned.

▸ **Remember:** Who you are is immeasurable.

AUTUMN

In "**NO PROBLEM, IT JUST GETS WORSE**," David says, "the problem, the stuckness, shifted from being what was wrong with me to being part of the creative process itself."

▸ **Reflect:** Where are you stuck in your life right now? What is the worst part of this stuckness? What if this stuckness is part of some larger creative process of unfolding? How might this be so?

▸ **Practice:** Next time you feel stuck, see what happens if you just allow yourself to be stuck. What happens if you don't try to get out, but allow yourself to be right where you are?

▸ **Remember:** Being stuck is part of the journey forward.

David tells the story of repairing the brick walkway at the temple in "**THE ROUGH PLACES PLAIN**." He writes of being surprised by the sense of well-being and accomplishment he felt after doing this, and being delighted by this seemingly unimportant action.

▸ **Reflect:** Think of the last time you felt a sense of pride and well-being upon completion of some mundane task. What were you doing? What is it that delighted you in the completion?

▸ **Practice:** Make a list of routine activities that give you pleasure or satisfaction. The list could include things as simple as cleaning up the kitchen or responding to email. Next time you do one of these activities, allow yourself to notice the simple pleasure of moving and doing and accomplishing.

▸ **Remember:** We can find fulfillment in the most ordinary activities.

In "BUDDHA COMES TO BOUNDLESS WAY TEMPLE" David says, "the universe responds when we clearly set out in some direction." He goes on to say: "I don't believe the universe has a personality or does really 'respond' in a way we can understand, but I have seen amazing things happen when we clarify our intention."

▸ **Reflect:** Do you believe the universe "responds" to us and our intentions? How does this belief or nonbelief impact what you choose to do and not do?

▸ **Practice:** Choose some area of your life where you would like to move forward. What is the dream you have that you would like to move toward? Think about it and imagine it in as much detail as you can. Now brainstorm a list of steps you could take to move toward this dream. Come up with as many as you can. Now look at this list and choose one that you can do in the next twenty-four hours. Do it.

▶ **Remember:** What we give our attention to gains energy and what we take our attention away from diminishes.

WINTER

In "**WANTING TO BE WILLIAM**," David writes of wishing he were William James, but then reflects "neither his many gifts nor the admiration of his peers and posterity saved him from the fullness and suffering of his human life."

▶ **Reflect:** Many of us sometimes feel that we should be like someone else—more intelligent, more emotional, less emotional, slimmer, more muscular... Where do you get caught in feeling you are less than you "should" be?

▶ **Practice:** Think about someone you admire. What is it about them that attracts you? What if you already possessed these qualities in yourself? What if you knew their actual experience of life was as complicated and sometimes confusing as yours?

▸ **Remember:** Don't compare your insides to someone else's outsides.

The balance between natural aliveness and hard work is the theme of "**TRUSTING THE ALIVENESS.**" The Buddha spoke of this as "right effort" and talked about the importance of the strings of a musical instrument being neither too tight nor too loose.

▸ **Reflect:** How do you know when you have the balance right in your life? What does it feel like for you when you try too hard? Or when you're not giving yourself fully to something important?

▸ **Practice:** What is some area of your life where you feel like you're trying too hard? Bring to mind some area in which you'd like to trust more and worry less. What is it you might trust more here? For one week, every time you do something in this area, begin by calling to mind this something you'd like to trust more.

▸ **Remember:** It doesn't have to be hard.

In "**GRUMBLING**," David reflects that as human beings we encounter many things that we don't like, that we wish were different—both inside and outside of ourselves. How we meet both the circumstances of our lives and meet our reaction to these circumstances determines the quality of our lives.

▶ **Reflect:** Every situation we encounter is an opportunity to wake up; what we need is already here. In what current situation of your life are you sure this is clearly not true? Consider the possibility that "even this" is it.

▶ **Practice:** Next time you are sure you are in the wrong place or notice yourself really objecting to some situation that is arising, stop for a moment and take a breath. Instead of continuing to "grumble," notice in detail what it is like to be here with your experience. What are the sensations and feelings of this place? What is here you have never noticed before?

▶ **Remember:** Even *this* is it.

SPRING

David appreciates the wonder of the "silent green shoots" of early spring in "**SPEAKING SOFTLY**." When we pay attention to what is around us, whether in a spring garden or on an urban street, we can notice that everything is constantly changing. We live out our lives in a world that is also living and when we meet this aliveness, we are changed in the interaction.

▶ **Reflect:** What aspect of the world especially speaks to you? How do you hear/feel/notice the world singing?

It might be in the beauty of nature or in the sound of a loved one's voice, in the motion of your own body in action or in the details of a really great story. Remember what you love and let yourself be touched by this memory.

▸ **Practice:** Take yourself to some place or some activity that delights you. Let yourself fully be where you are. Breathe in what is here for you. After a little while, consider what it is that this place has to teach you.

▸ **Remember:** The fullness of the universe is fully manifest in the particularness of each thing.

"**INSTRUCTIONS TO SELF FOR WANDERING**" is a brief reverie—a dreaming into impossible possibilities. The Zen tradition has a great appreciation for wandering, for journeying with no destination.

▸ **Reflect:** When have you had the opportunity to wander with no specific destination? What was that time like? What did you discover that you had not expected?

▸ **Practice:** Set aside a block of time—if possible, from one hour to a full day. Start out in some direction and see what you encounter. Let your feet guide you and your nose steer you. See what you haven't seen before. Don't get ahead of yourself. (You might want to take a camera with you to have a record of what you have not yet noticed.)

▶ **Remember:** When we give up our agenda, we find what we are looking for everywhere.

In "I FEEL LIKE A TOMATO SEEDLING," David imagines growth from the perspective of a tomato seed. He suggests that our growth as human beings does not happen in a linear and predictable way—that our lives do not always unfold in the manner and time we would like them to. Opening to the possibility that darkness and dissolution are part of life's forward movement can make the difficult times easier to bear.

▶ **Reflect:** What area of your life has unfolded in a way that is quite different from your expectation? What has been most difficult about this? What blessings have you encountered that you could not have expected?

▶ **Practice:** Pick an area of your life where you are most impatient for results. Notice what this impatience feels like. What is it you really want? What if you will never have it? What if you already have it?

▶ **Remember:** When it is dark, it is just dark, not a comment on you.

In the AFTERWORD, David writes of his wish for "greater appreciation of the grace of this beauty and love." We live in an astonishing world that is full of more surprises—more grace and more difficulty than we could imagine. Our job is not to control or even to manage, but to participate with and learn from what is already happening.

▸ **Reflect:** What do you love? Where do you see beauty?

▸ **Practice:** Spend a day consciously appreciating everything you encounter. Whether you perceive it as good or bad, meet it with a silent "thank you." If you notice that you find something particularly difficult to appreciate, you perhaps can even appreciate this difficulty. At the end of the day, take some time to appreciate yourself.

▸ **Remember:** Our lives can be an expression of our love.

About the Author

DAVID DAE AN RYNICK is a Zen teacher authorized in both the Korean Rinzai and the Japanese Soto lineages. He's a founding teacher of Boundless Way Zen, a rapidly expanding national network of Zen groups. Since 2003, Rynick has worked as a life and leadership coach, certified through the International Coaching Federation and the Coaches Training Institute. He provides coaching for a wide variety of individuals including religious leaders from several different faith traditions. Rynick has served as trainer and consultant to the Episcopal House of Bishops' peer coaching program since 2005. He has created and led numerous professional workshops and classes on leadership, systems thinking, coaching, meditation, diversity, and creativity, and has served as a faculty member at Cambridge College and the president of his Unitarian Universalist church. A former professional potter and improvisational dancer, he is also an avid landscape gardener as well as licensed as a Certified Maine Kayak Guide. Rynick holds a B.A. and an M.A.L.S. from Wesleyan University in Middletown, Connecticut. He is the resident teacher of the Boundless Way Zen Temple in Worcester, Massachusetts, where he lives with his wife, Melissa Myozen Blacker, also a Zen teacher. To contact David, go to www.DavidRynick.com.

About Wisdom Publications

WISDOM PUBLICATIONS is dedicated to offering works relating to and inspired by Buddhist traditions.

To learn more about us or to explore our other books, please visit our website at www.wisdompubs.org.

You can subscribe to our e-newsletter or request our print catalog online, or by writing to:

Wisdom Publications
199 Elm Street
Somerville, Massachusetts 02144 USA

You can also contact us at 617-776-7416, or info@wisdompubs.org.

Wisdom is a nonprofit, charitable 501(c)(3) organization and donations in support of our mission are tax deductible.

Wisdom Publications is affiliated with the Foundation for the Preservation of the Mahayana Tradition (FPMT).